Digital Totalitarianism

Digital Totalitarianism: Algorithms and Society focuses on important challenges to democratic values posed by our computational regimes: policing the freedom of inquiry, risks to the personal autonomy of thought, NeoLiberal management of human creativity, and the collapse of critical thinking with the social media fueled rise of conspiranoia.

Digital networks allow for a granularity and pervasiveness of surveillance by government and corporate entities. This creates power asymmetries where each citizen's daily 'data exhaust' can be used for manipulative and controlling ends by powerful institutional actors. This volume explores key erosions in our fundamental human values associated with free societies by covering government surveillance of library-based activities, cognitive enhancement debates, the increasing business orientation of art schools, and the proliferation of conspiracy theories in network media.

Scholars and students from many backgrounds, as well as policy makers, journalists and the general reading public will find a multidisciplinary approach to questions of totalitarian tendencies encompassing research from Communication, Rhetoric, Library Sciences, Art and New Media.

Michael Filimowicz is Senior Lecturer in the School of Interactive Arts and Technology (SIAT) at Simon Fraser University. He has a background in computer-mediated communications, audiovisual production, new media art, and creative writing. His research develops new multimodal display technologies and forms, exploring novel form factors across different application contexts, including gaming, immersive exhibitions, and simulations.

Algorithms and Society

Series Editor:
Dr Michael Filimowicz *is Senior Lecturer in the School of Interactive Arts and Technology (SIAT) at Simon Fraser University.*

As algorithms and data flows increasingly penetrate every aspect of our lives, it is imperative to develop sufficient theoretical lenses and design approaches to humanize our informatic devices and environments. At stake are the human dimensions of society which stand to lose ground to calculative efficiencies and performance, whether at the service of government, capital, criminal networks, or even a general mob concatenated in social media.

Algorithms and Society is a new series which takes a broad view of the information age. Each volume focuses on an important thematic area, from new fields such as software studies and critical code studies to more established areas of inquiry such as philosophy of technology and science and technology studies. This series aims to stay abreast of new areas of controversy and social issues as they emerge with the development of new technologies.

If you wish to submit a book proposal for the series, please contact Dr Michael Filimowicz michael_f@sfu.ca or Emily Briggs emily.briggs@tandf.co.uk

Digital Totalitarianism
Algorithms and Society
Edited by Michael Filimowicz

Privacy
Algorithms and Society
Edited by Michael Filimowicz

Systemic Bias
Algorithms and Society
Edited by Michael Filimowicz

Democratic Frontiers
Algorithms and Society
Edited by Michael Filimowicz

Deep Fakes
Algorithms and Society
Edited by Michael Filimowicz

For more information on the series, visit: https://www.routledge.com/Algorithms-and-Society/book-series/ALGRAS

Digital Totalitarianism
Algorithms and Society

**Edited by
Michael Filimowicz**

Routledge
Taylor & Francis Group

LONDON AND NEW YORK

First published 2022
by Routledge
4 Park Square, Milton Park, Abingdon, Oxon OX14 4RN

and by Routledge
605 Third Avenue, New York, NY 10158

Routledge is an imprint of the Taylor & Francis Group, an informa business

British Library Cataloguing-in-Publication Data
A catalogue record for this book is available from the British Library

Library of Congress Cataloging-in-Publication Data
Names: Filimowicz, Michael, editor.
Title: Digital totalitarianism : algorithms and society / edited by Michael Filimowicz.
Description: Abingdon, Oxon ; New York, NY : Routledge, 2022. | Series: Algorithms and society | Includes bibliographical references and index.
Identifiers: LCCN 2021052723 (print) | LCCN 2021052724 (ebook) | ISBN 9781032002415 (hardback) | ISBN 9781032002439 (paperback) | ISBN 9781003173304 (ebook)
Subjects: LCSH: Internet—Social aspects. | Privacy, Right of. | Intellectual freedom. | Conspiracy theories.
Classification: LCC HM851 .D545227 2022 (print) | LCC HM851 (ebook) | DDC 302.23/1—dc23/eng/20211230
LC record available at https://lccn.loc.gov/2021052723
LC ebook record available at https://lccn.loc.gov/2021052724

ISBN: 978-1-032-00241-5 (hbk)
ISBN: 978-1-032-00243-9 (pbk)
ISBN: 978-1-003-17330-4 (ebk)

DOI: 10.4324/9781003173304

Typeset in Times New Roman
by codeMantra

Contents

Contributors

Amanda C. Roth Clark holds an MLIS and PhD in Library and Information Studies from the University of Alabama. She is the Dean of the Library and Special Programs at Whitworth University in Spokane, Washington. Clark's research interests include architecture, artists' books, and library administration; master's degrees in addition to her MLIS include architectural history, theology, and progress toward an MBA.

Eleanor Dare works at Cambridge University of Faculty of Education. Eleanor is an academic and critical technologist with a PhD and an MSc in Arts and Computational Technologies from the Department of Computing, Goldsmiths. Eleanor was formerly Reader in Digital Media and Head of Programme for MA Digital Direction at the Royal College of Art.

Sophia E. Du Val obtained her MSLIS from Pratt Institute in New York City, with two advanced certificates in Archives and Museum Libraries. She currently serves as the Scholarly Communication Librarian at Whitworth University in Spokane, Washington, overseeing the university's Digital Commons platform and assisting with copyright and resource access. Her current research interests include zine and artists' book collection development, the memento mori, and collecting as historical narrative are primarily informed by her background in art history.

Raúl Rodríguez-Ferrándiz is Full Professor of Semiotics of Mass Communication and Transmedia Production at the University of Alicante, Spain. He has been academic coordinator of the Master of Communication and Creative Industries at the same University. He has published the books *Magics of fiction: Spoiler Warning!* (International Essay Prize 'Miguel de Unamuno', Bilbao, 2019,

Madrid, Devenir, 2020); *Masks of Lying: The New Post-Truth Disorder* (XXXV International Essay Prize 'Ciudad de Valencia', 2017; Valencia, Pre-Textos, 2018); *The Venal Muse: Production and Consumption of Industrial Culture* (International Essay Prize 'Miguel Espinosa', Murcia, Tres Fronteras, 2010); and *Apocalypse Show: Intellectuals, TV and End of the Millennium* (Madrid, Biblioteca Nueva, 2001). He has coordinated to the volume *The Controversy on Mass Culture in the Inter-War Period: A Critical Anthology* (University of Valencia, 2012).

Özüm Üçok-Sayrak, PhD, is Associate Professor at the Department of Communication and Rhetorical Studies at Duquesne University. Dr. Üçok-Sayrak has published papers on communication ethics and culture; embodiment and identity; mindfulness; and aesthetic communication. Her research interests include communication ethics, philosophy of communication, ethics and epistemology, contemplative education, and communicative construction of identity. Her work has been published in scholarly journals such as *Review of Communication, Journal of International and Intercultural Communication, Human Studies, Atlantic Journal of Communication,* and *Symbolic Interaction,* and in several edited books. She is the author of *Aesthetic Ecology of Communication Ethics: Existential Rootedness.*

Series Preface
Algorithms and Society

Michael Filimowicz

This series is less about what algorithms are and more about how they act in the world through "eventful" (Bucher, 2018, p. 48) forms of "automated decision making" (Noble, 2018, loc. 141), in which computational models are "based on choices made by fallible human beings" (O'Neil, 2016, loc. 126).

> Decisions that used to be based on human reflection are now made automatically. Software encodes thousands of rules and instructions computed in a fraction of a second.
>
> (Pasquale, 2015, loc. 189)

> If, in the industrial era, the promise of automation was to displace manual labor, in the information age it is to pre-empt agency, spontaneity, and risk: to map out possible futures before they happen so objectionable ones can be foreclosed and desirable ones selected.
>
> (Andrejevic, 2020, p. 8)

> [M]achine learning algorithms that anticipate our future propensities are seriously threatening the chances that we have to make possible alternative political futures.
>
> (Amoore, 2020, p. xi)

Algorithms, definable pragmatically as "a method for solving a problem" (Finn, 2017, loc. 408), "leap from one field to the next" (O'Neil, 2016, loc. 525). They are "*hyperobjects*: things with such broad temporal and spatial reach that they exceed the phenomenological horizon of human subjects" (Hong, 2020, p. 30). While in the main the technological systems taken up as volume topics are design solutions to problems for which there are commercial markets, organized communities, or claims of state interest, their power and ubiquity generate new problems for inquiry. The series will do its part to track this domain fluidity across its volumes and contest, through critique and investigation, their "logic of secrecy" (Pasquale, 2015, loc. 68), and "obfuscation" (loc. 144).

These new *social* (rather than strictly computational) problems that are generated can, in turn, be taken up by many critical, policy, and speculative discourses. At their most productive, such debates can potentially alter the ethical, legal, and even imaginative parameters of the environments in which the algorithms of our information architectures and infrastructures operate, as algorithmic implementations often reflect a "desire for epistemic purity, of knowledge stripped of uncertainty and human guesswork" (Hong, 2020, p. 20). The series aims to foster a general intervention in the conversation around these often "black boxed" technologies and track their pervasive effects in society.

> Contemporary algorithms are not so much transgressing settled societal norms as establishing new patterns of good and bad, new thresholds of normality and abnormality, against which actions are calibrated.
>
> (Amoore, 2020, p. 5)

Less "hot button" algorithmic topics are also of interest to the series, such as their use in the civil sphere by citizen scientists, activists, and hobbyists, where there is usually not as much discursive attention. Beyond private, state, and civil interests, the increasingly sophisticated technology-based activities of criminals, whether amateur or highly organised, deserve broader attention as now everyone must defend their digital identities. The information systems of companies and states conduct a general form of "ambient surveillance" (Pasquale, 2015, loc. 310), and anyone can be a target of a hacking operation.

Algorithms and Society thus aims to be an interdisciplinary series which is open to researchers from a broad range of academic backgrounds. While each volume has its defined scope, chapter contributions may come from many areas such as sociology, communications, critical legal studies, criminology, digital humanities, economics, computer science, geography, computational media and design, philosophy of technology, and anthropology, along with others. Algorithms are "shaping the conditions of everyday life" (Bucher, 2018, p. 158) and operate "at the intersection of computational space, cultural systems, and human cognition" (Finn, 2017, loc. 160), so the multidisciplinary terrain is vast indeed.

Since the series is based on the shorter Routledge Focus format, it can be nimble and responsive to emerging areas of debate in fast-changing technological domains and their sociocultural impacts.

REFERENCES

Amoore, L. (2020). *Cloud Ethics: Algorithms and the Attributes of Ourselves and Others*. Duke University Press.

Andrejevic, M. (2020). *Automated Media*. Taylor and Francis.

Bucher, T. (2018). *If...Then: Algorithmic Power and Politics*. Oxford University Press.

Finn, E. (2017). *What Algorithms Want: Imagination in the Age of Computing*. MIT Press. Kindle version.

Hong, S. H. (2020). *Technologies of Speculation: The Limits of Knowledge in a Data-Driven Society*. New York University Press.

Noble, S. U. (2018). *Algorithms of Oppression*. New York University Press. Kindle version.

O'Neil, C. (2016). *Weapons of Math Destruction*. Broadway Books. Kindle version.

Pasquale, F. (2015). *The Black Box Society*. Harvard University Press. Kindle version.

Volume Introduction

Michael Filimowicz

Digital Totalitarianism is investigated in this volume through specific degrading effects on the intellectual and creative freedoms of human beings in nominally democratic societies.

Chapter 1 – "Radical Resistance: Libraries, Defiance, and Data Surveillance" by Amanda C. Roth Clark and Sophia E. Du Val – takes up the meme-image of "radical, militant librarians" to highlight the new roles that libraries play with regard to safeguarding the privacy of their visitors' search and checkout histories which government agencies increasingly impinge upon. At stake are foundational citizens' rights of free access to information which are at the core of library science ethics.

Chapter 2 – "Urgent Ethical Issues in the Cognitive Enhancement Debate: Autonomy, Mental Privacy, and Freedom of Thought" by Özüm Üçok-Sayrak – takes up key debates of cognitive enhancement related to implantable devices and brain computer interfaces. Such technologies, installed at the neural level, do not simply enhance but also alter sensory, physical, and mental capabilities and pose new questions about traditional conceptions of the freedom and autonomy of thought and mental privacy.

Chapter 3 – "Impersonal Computing: from Art School to Business Hub in four decades" by Eleanor Dare – reviews art school trends in the Global North which, under NeoLiberal transformations and administrative models, are pushing art education away from long-established teaching traditions by taking up business school approaches. At the heart of these new pedagogical pressures are the interconnections between Computer Science and Business concepts that prioritize STEM and STEAM configurations of applied creativity.

Chapter 4 – "The Plandemic and its Apostles: Conspiracy Theories in Pandemic Mode" by Raúl Rodríguez-Ferrándiz – analyzes conspiracy theories and the "conspiranoia" associated with the COVID-19 pandemic as disseminated globally in social media. Building on Karl Popper's ideas, conspiracies are understood as "mythologies of modernity" which on the one hand share remarkable continuity with other conspiracies dating back centuries, but on the other hand take on new algorithm-driven potencies as part of our general information disorder.

Acknowledgment

The chapter summaries here have in places drawn from the authors' chapter abstracts, the full versions of which can be found in Routledge's online reference for the volume.

1 Radical Resistance

Libraries, Defiance, and Data Surveillance

*Amanda C. Roth Clark and
Sophia E. Du Val*

Radical, Militant Librarians

In the year 2001, shortly after the destruction of the Twin Towers, an FBI agent wrote in a series of emails about his exasperation with the "radical, militant librarians" who refused to comply with demands to turn over patron records to the Federal Bureau of Investigation. The criticism then was related to the FBI's use of secret warrants authorized under Section 215 of the USA PATRIOT Act to retrieve library user data. The efforts of these so-called "radical militant librarians" were on behalf of their patrons and their right to read what they wished safe from state surveillance or scrutiny. Such actions on the part of a significant contingent of library staff-persons nationwide subsequently "helped to influence the Congress in its vote to extend its debate on the renewal of the USA PATRIOT Act" (www.ala.org, January 17, 2006).

The moniker "radical, militant librarians" swept through the internet and remains anchored in online parlance to this day. Librarians were proud to wear badges, carry coffee mugs, and tote bags emblazoned with this title. What the "radical, militant librarians" were fighting against was possible and probable data profiling (Gellman & Dixman, 2011, p. 10), where searches, checkouts, and curiosity about outré topics could lead to state suspicion and inquiry, possibly implicating involvement in illegal activity. In short, the agent had identified something that the library community has held as a priority for decades, that patron privacy and the right to read whatever one wishes without observation or repercussions is indeed central to the ethos and work of the profession. The librarians perceived themselves as trendsetters for other disciplines in the safeguarding of rights regarding privacy, copyright, surveillance, data mining, and freedom—matters that are as relevant in today's digital age as they were decades ago, if not more so. This chapter addresses these and other important and contentious issues.

DOI: 10.4324/9781003173304-1

The Stacks (Don't) Have Eyes: The USA PATRIOT Act and Government Surveillance in the Library

Perhaps the most infamous threat to library patron privacy in recent memory has been the USA PATRIOT Act (Uniting and Strengthening America by Providing Appropriate Tools Required to Intercept and Obstruct Terrorism). Enacted in 2001 shortly after 9/11, the PATRIOT Act, specifically Section 215 and Section 505, gave enhanced powers to federal agents to request and collect library patrons' personal information, browsing habits, borrowing records, and more. This extended reach by the US government was immediately alarming to librarians due to its violations against the ethical standards of librarianship, standards that include but are not limited to intellectual freedom, information literacy, access, the universal right to free expression, and a broad host of other topics central to the American Library Association (ALA) Code of Ethics (1994) and the Library Bill of Rights (adopted in 1939 and last updated in 2019) (www.ala.org, August 19, 2021).

Furthermore, the PATRIOT Act included a nondisclosure provision that prohibited library workers from discussing if or when the FBI had requested information from them. Despite the reality that nearly every state had previously enacted laws protecting the confidentiality of library patrons, the state laws "are overridden or trumped by federal laws that allow federal agencies to seek library records. No federal or case law protects the privacy of library records" (Lambert et al., 2015, p. 3). Under the PATRIOT Act, a subpoena was no longer required for federal agents to obtain library patron records. Instead, a Foreign Intelligence Security Act (FISA) court order would suffice, and any record could be obtained for any reason, even without direct connection to open terrorism investigations. For the sake of dialectic, we should note that the PATRIOT Act was—from a centralized perspective—spurred to protect and defend the American public against terrorist threats, though this narrative has remained under continued debate within the academic community (Whitehead et al., 2002).

By turning the library into a location of suspicion where any patron's research could be collected and used against them, the PATRIOT Act eroded the ethical framework of privacy and intellectual freedom upon which libraries are built. The ALA was firmly entrenched by the twentieth century, but already by the nineteenth century, the association's work of librarianship was situated as a science in the eyes of the public (Lugya, 2014). By the twentieth century, librarians were adopting social science methods to determine what to collect, how to analyze user communities, and how to assess the information needs of those patron groups, all of which continues today and informs how librarians relate to and serve their patrons as well as what they choose to defend and support. The library studies landscape today is anchored in the social science tradition with additional ties to the utility and promotion of technology. Libraries today are focused on data sets, statistics, analyses, and arguments supported by quantifiable results. The posture of librarians to technology is one of freedom and openness rather than suspicion. "Librarians and book collectors are custodians of the transcript, the 'keepers of the Word' ...," writes Jesse Shera; rather than gatekeepers, they are defenders of open access to material, transcript, and the printed and digital word. Shera defines "the library as 'the memory of society,' the social cortex" (Shera, 1973, p. 91). Defense of access to this social cortex is paramount in the self-perception of the librarian. The library preserves and promotes information access; libraries can thus be viewed as containers of and promoters of human information and free access to that information. Without surveilled access to and use of these repositories of stored knowledge, the social risks are vast. With this hallowed worldview in mind, it is evident why librarians were alarmed by the aggressive and invasive arm of the PATRIOT Act. In hindsight, this seems to pale in comparison with present-day US Immigrations and Customs Enforcement (ICE) operations, which we will turn to shortly.

Defending Anonymity: Computers, Books, and Free Expression

Nancy Kranich, past president of the ALA, details the guild's concerns with the USA PATRIOT Act, particularly regarding how libraries play a unique role in the US in providing citizens a safe and free place to explore ideas, to, as she writes, "express opinions and to seek and receive information, the essence of a thriving democracy" (Burns, 2007, p. 158). It was with this conviction that many librarians tirelessly threw themselves into battle against the PATRIOT Act. Seeking to mitigate (or defy) government threats to patrons, these librarians reevaluated how personally identifying patron information was collected and then how it was stored and accessed in libraries. Some librarians on the website librarian.net took measures to circumnavigate the PATRIOT Act's nondisclosure provision by creating library signage that informs patrons about personal data collection. "The FBI has not been here. (Watch very closely for the removal of this sign)," one read (Foerstel, 2004, p. 79). Another announced: "We're sorry! Due to National

Security concerns, we're unable to tell you if your Internet surfing habits are being monitored by federal agents; please act appropriately" (Foerstel, 2004, p. 79). These examples highlight both the wit and humor when librarians who value patron anonymity confront threats to that anonymity. In a field often divided between "professional librarians" and "paraprofessionals," the library community has rallied under a unified banner of concern over this issue of state infringement.

Concerns did not arise only in the year 2001; they had emerged already in the 1980s when the FBI's Library Awareness Program became public (Rosen, 2000, p. 167). The Library Awareness Program, originating as early as the 1960s, involved tasking federal agents with asking librarians to keep tabs on patron records that seemed "suspicious," particularly in arenas of possible terrorist activity. Across the country, librarians refused to take part in the arbitrary surveillance of patrons. Paula Kaufman, librarian at Columbia University's Mathematics and Science Library, gave this statement in July 1988 to the House Subcommittee on Civil and Constitutional Rights:

> They asked us to report on who was reading what, and I refused to cooperate with them....They explained that libraries such as ours were often used by the KGB and other intelligence agents for recruiting activities....I continued to refuse to spy on our readers.
> (Foerstel, 2004, p. 13)

Righteous defiance has long been embedded in the DNA of librarians, the so-called "apostles of culture" (Garrison, 1979).

A textbook discussing the recent state-by-state laws protecting libraries from having to give over patron information and the ethical challenges within computing writ large offers this statement, "Librarians have a very strong belief in protecting the privacy of readers" (Baase, 1997, p. 44). Even as early as 1993—prior to the boom of the internet—librarians orchestrated conferences with themes such as "Computers, Freedom, and Privacy" (Baase, 1997, p. 80). The field of librarianship has long held that the hybrid culture of information and computers should be of paramount concern to the stewards of the profession, paramount because the computerized interface manipulates user experience (Emerson, 2014, pp. 32–33). Marshall McLuhan's prophetic adage, the "medium is the message," reminds us that while the physical book is a persistent and complex communication experience, the computer and digital interface likewise re-inform how humans access and internalize data (McLuhan & Fiore, 1967). Both computer and book are communicators of information; the experience of the digital and the analog go beyond content, beyond merely words or information. The digital book impacts the reception and interpretation of content; librarians have long been attuned to digital developments, both their pros and their cons. And even while libraries today may extol, rather than restrict or control, general terminal use in their facilities due to, for example, the surfing of pornographic content, libraries continue to uphold the need for patrons to view and research any topic area without governmental or institutional surveillance. Libraries also strive to move beyond proprietary designations of copyright and control even while negotiating with vendors over data privacy and excessive profit-driven proprietary access and sharing restrictions.

Privacy: Security and (Perceived) Rights

Persuasive author and friend of libraries Nicholas Carr insists that "as the older generations die, they take with them their knowledge of what was lost" (Carr, 2008, p. 233); we are wise to ask what is lost when we lose our privacy and succumb willingly to an easy surveillance in exchange for coupons, ease, and the illusory feeling of being "known." What Carr asks us to question and recall is that once memory is erased or obstructed, we can no longer question or challenge what we fail to recognize. When we give up our autonomy, we stand to lose our ability to question authority critically. For the library as an institution is at root about the storing and sharing of human memory, so that both what we have learned from the past and present may serve to refine and sharpen decisions and policy-making.

Rights or perceived rights to privacy have a long history in cultures deriving from Western European regions and the British Isles, expressed largely in the deliberations regarding natural law in the ancient past, and which surfaced with cultural force in the writings of Thomas Hobbes, John Locke, and John Stuart Mill (Glenn, 2003, pp. 16–18). Contemporary discussions of privacy home in on the value of the right to privacy and whether its worth can be counted as intrinsic (valued for its own sake) or instrumental (valued for how it can be used to achieve an end) (Himma & Tavani, 2008, p. 158). Herman T. Tavani, writing in *The Handbook of Information and Computer Ethics* (Himma & Tavani, 2008), renders support for the theories of Fried and Moor for the ways they both suggest that privacy must be thought of as simultaneously intrinsic and instrumental. Fried's conception of privacy is deeply human, emphasizing its necessity for building trust between individuals. "In Fried's scheme, we do not simply value privacy to achieve important human ends; rather, those ends would be inconceivable without privacy" (Himma & Tavani, 2008, p. 157). Moor likewise argues that privacy is both instrumental and intrinsic in its articulation of the value of security. Believing that security is critical for societal flourishing, he affirms "that as information technology insinuates itself more and more into our everyday lives, it increasingly threatens our privacy" (Himma & Tavani, 2008, p. 157). In the digital landscape of 2021, librarians continuously find themselves in the position of mediator between technology and user—even more so when the safety and privacy of library patrons hang in the balance.

The defense of privacy and liberty has been long upheld by libraries, as noted in the 1955 book *Right to Read*, which recounts early librarian fights against censorship in the Library Bill of Rights which stated that books "should not be proscribed or removed from library shelves because of partisan or doctrinal disapproval" (Blanshard, 1955, p. 69). Moreover, concern over what persons are learning in libraries has been a concern to authorities during many phases of US history, particularly in postwar America (Blanshard, 1955, p. 113). Unlike other sectors of society, librarians resist passing judgment on a patron's possible intent to commit a crime based on their reading or searching habits within the library (Ahia & Martin, 1993, p. 9). While, unlike other professions, there are written or unwritten agreements between parties, the right to privacy between library and patron is one defended outside of and beyond contract (Ahia & Martin, 1993, p. 10). It is culturally and ethically embedded in the very profession of librarianship.

Balance as a principle of library access is a central issue protecting privacy and the opening up of information (Forester & Morrison, 1995, p. 131). In the opening example featuring the irritation of the now-legendary FBI agent, the patron record was desired for the potential intelligence it housed and was safeguarded to protect the patron. This decision to safeguard patron records points to the question of balance—a record of books may just as easily be a useful tool to the patron themselves in recalling what they have read as it is when used by law officials to determine areas of interest to that patron, and whether those interests seem to support terrorism or illegal activity. Privacy remains a controversial topic when it appears connected to public security and discussions of the greater good over that of the individual. As Donald Normam notes, "The roadblocks are political….they lead to political tension between those who want to safeguard their private information from others and the governments that are concerned about the use of these same technologies by organized crime, terrorists, and other miscreants" (Norman, 1998, p. 257). Typically, the librarian defends rights to access, choosing not to err on the side of restriction, for as it is oft-purported information wants to be free (Wagner, 2010). As the authors of *Right to Privacy* state, "privacy" is not mentioned in the constitution directly, and yet not only do persons in the US consider it a fundamental right, librarianship as a field has made it a point to support privacy (Alderman & Kennedy, 1995, p. xiii). US law has and continues to lag behind the speed at which cyber security is evolving (Alderman & Kennedy, 1995, p. xvi). While written in the twentieth century, this book looks ahead to the concerns looming even then on the horizon. At the time of writing, it was noted that the cell phone lacked security and that only the landline was secure; the authors conclude that persons must "change [their] idea of what we can reasonably expect to keep private" (Alderman & Kennedy, 1995, p. 332). The questions are: should we allow our privacy to be violated either for the sake of perceived safety or for advertising and convenience; how much should we welcome, allow, or tolerate such sale of our privacy; and at what cost should we willingly relinquish our own identity at the altar of convenience and narcissism? Twenty-six years later, these concerns have only multiplied.

Big Data and the Sale of Patron Information

Data storage and privacy are of utmost concern to librarians. With the increasing ability to store massive numbers of files on computers for an apparently indefinite period of time, which can then be transferred and searched, privacy concerns grow more acute (Barger, 2008, p. 9). Born-digital data, like all electronic information, we might argue, "seems to resist ownership" (Lanham, 1993, p. 19). That which was penned by hand, published in small runs, and distributed by people to people, was at every step linked to concepts of ownership, passed hand to hand, person to person. Digital data, and digital media, obfuscates ownership, and is often written and posted anonymously online and then read alone, unobserved, under "incognito" mode, caches wiped after use. Digital information, as defined by these characteristics, seems to scurry away from the arena of that which is "owned" or claimed. The recent rise of fake news and its shockingly devastating fallout speaks to this very point. Michel Foucault has postulated that "We can easily imagine a culture where discourse would circulate without any need for an author. Discourses, whatever their status, form, or value, and regardless of our manner of handling them, would unfold in a pervasive anonymity" (Foucault, 1969, p. 314). Foucault thus prophetically described the anonymity of the internet, the curation of big data, and "ownerless" information. The proliferation of seemingly anonymous information lends itself to the profit of fake news. In this era of the false, the uninformed, and that of rampant conspiracy theory, the reading public appears less capable than our forbearers to discern truth or lies in text (Sullivan, 2018). Much of this debate over privacy limits, openness, freedom, and rights rest in the definition of "ownership" (Brown, 1990, pp. 115–116), with librarians not viewing the library institution as "owning" any patron data, but rather serving as matchmaker between patron and information, allowing the patron to gain their own knowledge and, ultimately, wisdom. Once considered shushing gatekeepers, the librarian today is envisaged as a professional who connects people with ideas; even the books, ebooks, and journals housed in the institutions are not "owned" but stewarded. Integrated library systems have generated software with an algorithm for patron data protection. We must question, however, whether present conundrums lie in the machines collecting information or the groups that wish to use the data collected (Kearns & Roth, 2020, pp. 190–192). Or as Jeff Scheible has cautioned, we must better understand the technologies we employ and how we use them, avoiding that trap of expecting digital inventions to solve our most complicated human challenges (Scheible, 2015, p. 138). It seems rather that at times these smart technologies only further complete those problems. As Lori Emerson asserts in her book, *Reading Writing Interfaces*, "This assumption that tools are inherently neutral, neither good nor bad, is precisely what separates twentieth-century computer-generated writing from twenty-first-century reading-writing" (Emerson, 2014, p. 177) and that of, in our consideration here, patron data collection; we should be increasingly wary, perhaps, of the false neutrality of information collection.

Books such as C. A. Pickover's *Visions of the Future* envision many possible digital futures, some likely, others fanciful (see Pickover, 1994). The information held in our social media profiles is used by marketers to attempt to sell us products. Algorithms determine our likes and steer us toward more products and ultimately toward someone else turning a profit, even on apps such as TikTok. But when we are "in the computer," our personal information can be used against us (Tehranian, 1990, pp. 130–131). With the mining of big data, nightly uploads, and over-watching software, safeguarding patron records presents new challenges as technology evolves. What patrons check out and view online is captured and—as we are finding—harvested and sold to groups such as ICE. Librarians—long the defenders of immigration rights and only recently resolving to remove the term "illegal alien" as a cataloging designation—would thus find participation in the deportation of those seeking refuge anathema to the overarching goals of the profession.

Unfortunately, the commodification of user data is not a new phenomenon. As early as the 1980s, big data group LexisNexis (purchased by RELX Group, parent company of academic publisher Reed Elsevier, in 1994 for over $1 billion) became embroiled in a class-action lawsuit when it was discovered that the company had been purchasing, packaging, and selling the credit information and Social Security numbers of millions of Americans (Henderson, 1999, p. 24). The company agreed to remove anyone's name from their databases upon request, and removed all Social Security numbers.

Most recently, RELX Group and fellow data conglomerate Thomson Reuters, itself now facing charges of selling consumer data without consent, have been profiting from selling user data gleaned from their products to government agencies like ICE. These corporations, while still involved in media and publishing, have pivoted from their original business interests to data harvesting in order to maximize profits in the digital age. "Thomson Reuters has been even more successful than RELX in profiting from ICE surveillance," notes Sarah Lamdan, legal research librarian and Professor of Law at City University of New York (CUNY) School of Law, "[It] has signed at least three contracts to provide ICE with surveillance services totaling over $46 million" (Lamdan, 2019b, p. 277). The convergence of content and surveillance services under single vendors, including LexisNexis' ThreatMetrix (owned by RELX Group) and Thomson Reuters' Consolidated Lead Evaluation and Reporting (CLEAR), poses an ethical dilemma for libraries whose funds now support systems that violate the individual right to privacy and promote discriminatory policing practices perpetrated against minorities and immigrants (SPARC, 2021). These vendors provide high-quality legal and news content that patrons have need of, but also now provide personal data to government agencies that those agencies might otherwise not have a right to compile on their own (C. Hill, personal communication, July 19, 2021). It is worth quoting at length Sarah Lamdan's explanation of how RELX and Thomson Reuters perform their data brokerage:

> As commercial data brokers, RELX Group and Thomson Reuters aggregate and resell individualized data. At the beginning of the information supply chain, individuals provide their personal information to various government entities and share their online consumer data and location data with software companies who

sell the bundled data to firms specializing in data tracking. Powerful data aggregators like Thomson Reuters and RELX Group then purchase and consolidate the information held by individual data tracking firms, along with further data gleaned from public records, to create an informational mosaic describing millions of different people in great detail. Through this supply chain, Thomson Reuters and RELX Group hold stores of personal data including public records held by local, state, and federal governments, online data including individuals' use of social networks, blogs, chat rooms, lists of relatives and associates, and any other data they can purchase or collect. These brokers then sell these detailed individualized databases to businesses and law enforcement.

(Lamdan, 2019b, p. 275)

Surveillance, especially surveillance of immigrants, "offers Thomson Reuters and RELX Group new sources of income as selling print resources and online case databases becomes less lucrative" (Lamdan, 2019b, p. 255). Despite public outcry and boycotts from the librarian community, the shadow of data surveillance is ingrained in libraries' databases. "Surveillance researcher Wolfie Christl has reported ThreatMetrix tracking code is now embedded in the ScienceDirect website, raising serious questions about what patron information is being collected and toward what purposes" (SPARC, 2021, n.p.). Furthermore, the consolidation of library vendors gives librarians fewer choices when it comes to implementing database products. This lack of leverage, says Lamdan, leaves libraries with no other option but to purchase products from RELX Group or Thomson Reuters (Lamdan, 2019a, n.p.). It is a woeful predicament: protect patron privacy by resisting the ever-increasing threat of predatory information capitalism or sideline patron information needs by deliberately leaving gaping holes in library research collections. Those within the library profession increasingly find themselves caught in expanding vender monopolies within the industry, and squeezed between wishing to provide those resources desired by their patrons and being concerned with the ethics (or lack thereof) of vendors who often hold nearly exclusive rights over content, content which is then sold at rapidly increasing and extortionary rates.

Censorship: Surveillance and Creeping Apathy

Among those things that librarians fight against, in addition to resisting surveillance and an invasion of privacy, is censorship. A term somewhat difficult to define, censorship is "an idea [that] always engages our prejudices, penetrates to the dim regions where our manners and mores take form, and shapes our attitude to the rule of law" (McCormick & MacInnes, 1962, p. xiii). But why is this the particular concern of librarians? McCormick and MacInnes suggest that "in its complexities, the manifold guises of censorship trick us into apathy" (McCormick & MacInnes, 1962, p. xix). As a whole, librarians refuse such apathy, rendering consistent resistance to patron surveillance.

Since George Orwell's prophetic novel *1984* was released, many have been uncomfortable with being labeled anything akin to "Big Brother" or viewed as apathetic to infringements upon intellectual freedom and the right for privacy (Forester & Morrison, 1995, p. 152). And yet, as our personal technological devices offer us more algorithmic conveniences, it seems that we are slowly losing our standards or concerns regarding surveillance. That which is helpful is often more generously tolerated. The Federal Communications Commission (FCC) historically has had the ability to regulate communication by radio and wire, opening up questions about ebooks and other digital content (Paxton, 2000, p. 130). For further discussion of surveillance, see Glenn Greenwald, *No Place to Hide: Edward Snowden, the NSA, and the U.S. Surveillance State*. New York: Metropolitan Books, 2014.

The ethics of being surveilled and in-name-only privacy continue to be of central concern to the librarian community. "Surveillance generates information, which is often stored in record systems and used for new purposes," Daniel Solove warns us. "Being watched and inhibited in one's behavior is only one part of the problem; the other dimension is that the data is warehoused for unknown future uses" (Solove, 2004, p. 42). The librarian defends against unknown future uses by purging data, commonly as an automatic purge of information each evening, erasing the past of what a patron has read or searched. Reg Whitaker makes a compelling argument that a rejection of surveillance is not born out of fear that one has "something to hide," but rather the fear that there is nowhere to hide (Whitaker, 1999, p. 158). A basic assumption inverted becomes a Kafkaesque nightmare.

Intersections with Copyright and Access

While this chapter cannot address the overlapping issues concerning copyright and a greater understanding of such rights in general, a wealth of literature exists in the area of copyright and access. See, for example, Philip Doty, "Privacy, Reading, and Trying Out Identity" (Aspray & Doty, p. 2001). Michael Lynch gets at the heart of what motivates some librarians to protect unmonitored internet access among patrons, because as an epistemic resource "if you start limiting access, you not only contribute to epistemic inequality, you contribute to inequality, period" (Lynch, 2017, p. 145). What is at stake is not just privacy or rights, but the very foundation of access, which is the foundation of information.

Gary Hall has argued that we must scrutinize even those organizations striving to do good if they are working within assumptions predicated on a profit-driven, law-based publishing model. Creative Commons, for example, falls within the passive structures that commence from a capitalistic, copy-"right" model. To combat this, Hall suggests a more radical departure such as "copyleft" should strive even further in being "copyfarleft" or "copygift" (Hall, 2016). Hall targets a nexus of peer-reviewed journals, noting that they revolve centrally around the vetting of academics for promotion, funding, and ultimately continued employability. He attacks the monetization of personal data—an annual billion-dollar industry within the US—which is entangled with data analytics being mined both for profit and within the academy for careerism. The academy is so entrenched and dependent on these systems that even for those promoting open access models, many are still confined by the limitations imposed by a profit-driven, legally minded industry. While librarians wish to gather and interpret patterns aggregated by big data, we must pause to consider who has access to such data and what they wish to use it for.

Librarians are proud of their commitment to fostering an inclusive, equitable environment in the library. Guided by the values as described in the Library Bill of Rights outlined by the ALA, the guild of librarians actively pursues equity in all manners in which it provides services to its community members. Equity of access, a value that has been especially influential over the course of librarianship in the US, ensures the flourishing of intellectual freedom. "The historical continuity of librarianship" affirm authors Jaeger, Green Taylor, and Gorham:

> is not tied to the objects that contain information, like books records, computers, and e-books. The continuity lies in providing access to information, ensuring that patrons can use and understand the information, and advocating for the unmet needs of their patrons.
>
> (Jaeger, et al., 2015, p. 4)

Public libraries are unique spaces in a society of commodification and consumerism. They are free, open to all, and able to provide important social services to vulnerable populations. While librarians sometimes struggle to meet the needs of the community, they work tirelessly to ensure that access to library services and technologies remains unimpeded, equitable, and safe.

Author-activist Gary Hall encourages readers to struggle against systemic copyright that fails to truly empower either the author or the reader seeking access. Hall states, "This is why I am suggesting perhaps acting something like pirate philosophers: because a responsible ethical, as opposed to moralistic, approach to piracy would not presume to know what it is in advance" (Hall, 2016, p. 141). In short, he prompts resisting an antiquated system of control that exploits rather than supports the individual. Hall's advice, furthermore, supports those actions taken by the "radical, militant librarian," who acted, as he suggests, when confronting impossible decisions, "responsibly, and with as much care and thought, as possible" (Hall, 2016, p. 117). Long-standing concerns within the library community revolve around the unfortunate reality that patrons are increasingly unempowered and victimized by profit-driven or power-driven data collection fueled by powerful analytics.

Conclusion

In 2013, Michael Zimmer described the challenges associated with "the Faustian Bargain of Library 2.0" (Zimmer, 2013, p. 46). He asked, "How do we integrate...useful Web 2.0 technologies into the sphere of the library without compromising patron privacy and the values professional librarians have committed themselves to protecting?" (Zimmer, 2013, p. 46). The term Web 2.0, coined in the mid-2000s by Tim O'Reilly and Dale Dougherty, characterized a new "data-rich" era of the internet—one of interactivity, collaboration, and heightened user experience (Zimmer, 2013, p. 46). However, this breaking dawn of a more personalized internet necessitated the concession of more of users' personal information than before. Our thoughts, opinions, photography, work history, and hobbies quickly became the ultimate currency in the socialscape of the new internet—and librarians wondered how to harness the power of online interpersonal connections to facilitate patron-library interaction ethically without compromising patron privacy. "Conceptually," questions Zimmer, "what is the primary value within the librarian ethic that should drive policy: access or privacy?" (Zimmer, 2013, p. 53).

Librarians are critically aware of the fine line between access and privacy. While the myriad technological innovations of the twenty-first century may offer convenience and connection, consumer data protection is not a guarantee. As summarized by Tavani in *The Handbook of Information and Computer Ethics*, four particularly relevant privacy concerns resulting from contemporary technological developments include risks associated with cookie technology, threats to personal identifying information vis-à-vis data mining, workplace surveillance technology, and geo-location privacy violations from radio-frequency identification (RFID) (Tavani, 2008, pp. 151–156). Librarians are very much aware of these and other threats to privacy that loom large in the age of algorithms, and they work to mitigate hazards to patron privacy by working with vendors to increase patron privacy protections in digital products, identifying security risks in the products they subscribe to, and teaching instructional sessions on maximizing data privacy at home (Pedley, 2020, pp. 145–151).

For the initiated, the contents of this chapter should come as no surprise. As Marilyn Johnson notes, librarians have long been militantly radical when it comes to rights and knowledge; information that wants to be free (Johnson, 2010, p. 12). While shirking—or reveling in—stereotypes, librarians marshal behind their chosen causes with implacable verve and single-minded fact-gathering that makes them part-lawyer, part-hacker, and all cyber-sleuth. It is no wonder, then, that librarians staunchly defend patron privacy and oppose library surveillance. This bespectacled, watchful, well-read and tattooed army of critical thinkers is bent on protecting truth like few other professions today, and they do so largely without excess profit, kudos, or celebration.

Stephens-Davidowitz is incorrect when he claims that "in the age of the internet, not owning a library card is no longer embarrassing" (Stephens-Davidowitz & Pinker, 2017, p. 106); the authors of this chapter suggest that in an age of IP address footprints as well as private and government surveillance, the ability to enter a library and use anonymous terminals to browse the internet and then check out a book—the record of which will be almost immediately erased—is of global importance, and no mere matter of social "embarrassment." Quite the opposite.

Works Cited

Ahia, C. E., & Martin, D. (1993). *The danger-to-self-or-others exception to confidentiality* (Vol. 8). American Counseling Association.

ALA. (January 17, 2006). *ALA introduces "Radical, Militant Librarian" button*. American Library Association. https://www.ala.org/news/news/pressreleases2006/january2006/radicalmilitantbutton.

ALA. (June 30, 2006). *Library bill of rights.* American Library Association. http://www.ala.org/advocacy/intfreedom/librarybill

ALA. (October 23, 2015). *Access to library resources and services.* American Library Association. http://www.ala.org/advocacy/intfreedom/access.

Alderman, E., & Kennedy, C. (1995). *The right to privacy.* Alfred A. Knopf.

Aspray, W., & Doty, P. (Eds.) (2001). *Privacy in America: Interdisciplinary perspectives.* Scarecrow Press.

Baase, S. (1997). *A gift of fire: Social, legal, and ethical issues in computing.* Prentice Hall.

Barger, R. N. (2008). *Computer ethics: A case-based approach.* Cambridge University Press.

Blanshard, P. (1955). *The right to read: The battle against censorship.* Beacon Press.

Brown, G. (1990). *The information game: Ethical issues in a microchip world.* Humanities Press International.

Burns, K. (Ed.). (2007). *Censorship.* Greenhaven Press.

Carr, N. G. (2008). *The big switch: Rewiring the world, from Edison to Google* (1st ed.). W.W. Norton.

Doty, P. (2011). Privacy, reading, and trying out identity: The Digital Millennium Copyright Act and technological determinism. In W. Aspray & P. Doty (Eds.), *Privacy in America: Interdisciplinary Perspectives* (pp. 211–246). Scarecrow Press.

Emerson, L. (2014). *Reading writing interfaces: From the digital to the bookbound.* University of Minnesota Press.

Foerstel, H. N. (2004). *Refuge of a scoundrel: The Patriot Act in libraries.* Libraries Unlimited.

Forester, T., & Morrison, P. (1995). *Computer ethics: Cautionary tales and ethical dilemmas in computing* (2nd ed., 3rd reprint). MIT Press.

Foucault, M. (1969). What is an author? In D. Preziosi (Ed.), *The art of art history: A critical anthology* (pp. 299–314). Oxford University Press.

Garrison, D. (1979). *Apostles of culture: The public librarian and American society, 1876–1920.* University of Wisconsin Press.

Gellman, R., & Dixman, P. (2011). *Online privacy: A reference handbook.* ABC-CLIO.

Glenn, R. A. (2003). *The right to privacy: Rights and liberties under the law.* ABC-CLIO.

Greenwald, G. (2014). *No place to hide: Edward Snowden, the NSA, and the U.S. surveillance state.* Metropolitan Books.

Hall, G. (2016). *Pirate philosophy: For a digital posthumanities.* MIT Press.

Henderson, H. (1999). *Privacy in the information age.* Facts on File.

Himma, K. E., & Tavani, H. T. (Eds.) (2008). *The handbook of information and computer ethics.* Wiley.

Jaeger, P. T., Taylor, N. G., & Gorham, U. (2015). *Libraries, human rights, and social justice: Enabling access and promoting inclusion.* Rowman & Littlefield.

Johnson, M. (2010). *This book is overdue!: How librarians and cybrarians can save us All* (1st ed.). Harper.

Kearns, M., & Roth, A. (2020). *The ethical algorithm: The science of socially aware algorithm design.* Oxford University Press.

Lambert, A. D., Parker, M., & Bashir, M. (2015). Library patron privacy in jeopardy: An analysis of the privacy policies of digital content vendors. *Proceedings of the Association for Information Science and Technology, 52*(1), 1–9.

Lamdan, S. (2019a, November 13). *Librarianship at the crossroads of ICE surveillance.* In the Library with the Lead Pipe. https://www.inthelibrarywiththeleadpipe.org/2019/ice-surveillance/.

Lamdan, S. (2019b). When Westlaw fuels ICE surveillance: Legal ethics in the era of big data policing. *N.Y.U. Review of Law and Social Change, 43*(2), 255–293.

Lanham, R. A. (1993). *The electronic word: Democracy, Technology, and the Arts.* The University of Chicago Press.

Lugya, F. K. (2014). What counts as a science and discipline in library and information science? *Library Review 63*, 138–155.

Lynch, M. P. (2017). *The internet of us: Knowing more and understanding less in the age of big data.* Liveright.

McCormick, J., & MacInnes, M. (Eds.). (1962). *Versions of censorship: An anthology* (1st ed.). Anchor Books.

McLuhan, M., & Fiore, Q. (1967). *The medium is the massage: An inventory of effects.* Bantam Books.

Norman, D. A. (1998). *The invisible computer: Why good products can fail, the personal computer is so complex, and information appliances are the solution.* MIT Press.

Paxton, M. (2000). *Censorship.* Greenwood Press.

Pedley, P. (2020). *A practical guide to privacy in libraries.* Facet tPublishing.

Pickover, C. A., (Ed.). (1994). *Visions of the future: Art, technology, and computing in the twenty-first century.* (Rev. ed.). St. Martin's Press.

Rosen, J. (2000). *The unwanted gaze: The destruction of privacy in America* (1st ed.). Random House.

Scheible, J. (2015). *Digital shift: The cultural logic of punctuation.* University of Minnesota Press.

Shera, J. H. (1973). For whom do we conserve, or what can you do with a Gutenberg bible. In J. H. Shera (Ed.), *Knowing books and men: Knowing computers, too* (pp. 79–92). Libraries Unlimited.

Solove, D. J. (2004). *The digital person: Technology and privacy in the information age.* New York University Press.

SPARC. (2021, April 9). *Addressing the alarming systems of surveillance built by library vendors.* SPARC*. https://sparcopen.org/news/2021/addressing-the-alarming-systems-of-surveillance-built-by-library-vendors/.

Stephens-Davidowitz, S., & Pinker, S. (2017). *Everybody Lies: Big data, new data, and what the internet reveals about who we really are.* Dey St.

Sullivan, M. C. (2018). Why librarians can't fight fake news. *Journal of Librarianship and Information Science.* Retrieved from https://doi.org/10.1177/0961000618764258.

Tehranian, M. (1990). *Technologies of power: Information machines and democratic prospects.* Ablex.

Wagner, R. Polk (2010). *Information wants to be free: Intellectual property and the mythologies of control.* University of Pennsylvania.

Whitaker, R. (1999). *The end of privacy: How total surveillance is becoming a reality.* New Press.

Whitehead, John W. et al. (2002). Forfeiting 'enduring freedom' for 'homeland security:' A constitutional analysis of the USA Patriot Act and the justice department's anti-terrorism initiatives. *American University Law Review, 51*(6), 1081–1133.

Zimmer, M. (2013). Patron privacy in the 2.0 era. *Journal of Information Ethics, 22*(1), 44–59.

2 Urgent Ethical Issues in the Cognitive Enhancement Debate

Autonomy, Mental Privacy, and Freedom of Thought

Özüm Üçok-Sayrak

This essay invites a pause to consider several ethical questions that arise regarding the ongoing debate and research on cognitive enhancement, specifically focusing on the potential implications of implantable brain devices and brain-computer interfaces (BCI) on autonomy, mental privacy, and freedom of thought. I first start with offering background context to frame this essay through Rushkoff's (2019) discussion on figure/ground reversals in human inventions and Lanier's (2010) warnings on the deeply transformative effects of the designs and structures of digital technologies on the perceptions, identities, and interactions of people. Next, I explore the multifaceted strategies and technologies of cognitive enhancement, underlining their differences, side effects, and implications to have an informed debate on the heated and risky topic of cognitive enhancement and to avoid the trivialization of the technological forms of enhancement such as brain implants. Third, I offer a discussion on emerging biotechnological cognitive enhancement strategies such as invasive brain implants and BCI that not only enhance but *alter* sensory and physical capabilities of human beings through transgression of biological boundaries by technological means, which is an alarmingly controversial issue that we cannot afford to trivialize. I conclude by highlighting the life-saving importance of our human capacity to be able to take intervals within the digital that we already are embedded in towards resisting "thoughtlessness" (Arendt, 1958) as a crucial preventative measure before diving into anything new that becomes techno-scientifically possible yet might be murderous.

Figure/Ground Reversals in the Digital Media Environment

In *Team Human*, Rushkoff (2019) writes about figure/ground reversals regarding human inventions: Instead of the invention serving humans,

DOI: 10.4324/9781003173304-2

the opposite starts to happen and humans start serving the invention. That is, humans lose track of figure and ground and become enslaved in the systems they invent. "When we lose track of figure and ground, we forget who is doing what for whom, and why. We risk treating people as objects" (Rushkoff, 2019, p. 44). A recent example of this is related to smartphone use along with social media. Rather than the smartphone and its applications serving humans, many people get absorbed in or even addicted to the various services a smartphone offers with significant consequences of living a mostly virtual life leading to depression, isolation, decrease in empathy, and increased numbers of suicides, especially affecting young adults.

Rushkoff (2019) offers several examples to illustrate figure/ground reversals. Money, for instance, "was originally invented to store value and enable transactions... Today, the acquisition of money itself has become the central goal, and the marketplace just a means of realizing that goal" (Rushkoff, 2019, p. 44). In recent years, a powerful and dangerous figure/ground reversal takes place in the digital media environment with destructive consequences for community and connection: The role of the human and the instrument/machine gets replaced.

"If we don't truly know what something is programmed to do, chances are it is programming us" (Rushkoff, 2019, p. 50). A seemingly simple yet powerful example that Rushkoff (2019) offers is memes, which are more than just some catchy slogans but a form of code. The function of a meme is to be reproduced by stimulating the human to share it through arousing excitement, panic, rage, or other intensified emotional response (Rushkoff, 2019). The meme is "engineered to infect the human mind and then to turn that person into a replicator of the virus" (Rushkoff, 2019, p. 50). The meme orders to be reproduced, and the human obeys, turning the human to an instrument. One might question this statement, highlighting the autonomy and choices human beings have. The next section and the remainder of this essay aims to explore the question of autonomy that human beings willingly or unwillingly surrender in a digital age, and the implications of this compliance on the debate on cognitive enhancement and issues related to mental privacy and integrity, freedom of thought, and decision-making.

Fragmentation by Design

A pioneer of virtual reality technology, Jaron Lanier, cautions that as a developer of digital technologies, he is always reminded of "how small changes in the details of a digital design can have profound unforeseen effects on the experiences of humans who are playing with it" (Lanier, 2010, p. 4). Lanier (2010) explains that a seemingly trivial change such as the ease of use of a button can sometimes lead to major changes in behavioral patterns. An example Lanier offers comes from a research done by Stanford University researchers Yee et al. (2009) who demonstrated that changing the height in one's avatar transforms self-esteem and social self-perception both in online and offline interactions.

Lanier (2010) writes in a very straightforward fashion on the role of inventors of digital technologies and programmers as social engineers:

> We make up extensions to your being, like remote eyes and ears (webcams and mobile phones) and expanded memory (the world of details you can search for online). These become the structures by which you connect to the world and other people. These structures in turn can change how you conceive of yourself and the world. We tinker with your philosophy by direct manipulation of your cognitive experience, not indirectly, through argument.
>
> (p. 6)

As a programmer who is directly involved in creating the designs and structures of digital technologies that shape perceptions, identities, and interactions of people, Lanier (2010) underlines the importance of discussions on the interactions between humans and technology. Raising crucial questions on the various kinds of impact different digital technologies and media designs have in stimulating "different potentials in human nature" (Lanier, 2010, p. 5), Lanier cautions about the shaping of the entire future of human experience.

The "widespread practice of fragmentary, impersonal communication has demeaned interpersonal interaction" (Lanier, 2010, p. 4). The new generation who has normalized and adopted the impersonal, fragmented forms of communication that digital technologies facilitate have "a reduced expectation of what a person can be, and of who each person can become" (p. 4). A significant example that illustrates the reduction of embodied people to fragments of information is the digital representations of self and relationships on social networking sites that many people, especially young adults, spend much time and energy to keep managing. Whoever is able to create the most successful online fictions about themselves and their lives become the winners of this illusory world, and whoever takes a wrong turn in these digital tunnels risk being humiliated, cancelled, and trolled. It can be an unforgiving world with serious consequences related to isolation, alienation, anxiety, depression, self-harm, and suicide, especially in the lives of adolescents and young adults (Jacob et al., 2017; Keles et al., 2020; Kross et al., 2013; Tobin et al., 2015; Twenge, 2019).

An illustrative example regarding the consequences of the reduction of human beings to bits of information, and the process and experience of communication to information exchange, is the platform of Twitter that demands simplicity due to the limitation of characters. Ott (2017) writes that "Twitter is structurally ill equipped to handle complex content" (p. 61) due to the character limit. Furthermore, tweeting requires little effort, forethought, or reflection. "Tweets are often sparked by an affective charge that they transfer through the social network…" (Ott, 2017, p. 61) and trains users to speak impulsively. Combined with the informal and depersonalized aspects of Twitter along with simplicity and impulsivity, it does not come as a surprise to find intolerant, degrading, aggressive, insulting forms of discourse that undermine civility on Twitter, including the ease of canceling which has become a trend on Twitter. These patterns of interaction also extend to other domains of communication, including face-to-face interactions, shaping the public space.

I offer the introductory discussion above as a context for the following examination of the ongoing debate on cognitive enhancement. Rushkoff's (2019) discussion on figure/ground reversals in human inventions and Lanier's (2010) warnings on the transformative effects of the designs and structures of digital technologies on the perceptions, identities, and interactions of people serve as critical reference points to keep in mind as we move onto the cognitive enhancement-related inquiry below.

Strategies of Cognitive Enhancement and Urgent Ethical Questions

In a recent article titled "Hacking the brain: Dimensions of cognitive enhancement," Dresler et al. (2019) write: "In an increasingly complex information society, demands for cognitive functioning are growing steadily." Dresler et al. (2019) explain that to meet the challenges to acquire and maintain cognitive skills for improved performance in a world that is fast changing, an increasing number of people started to experiment with strategies to overcome the natural limitations of human cognitive capacity. Enhancement refers to "interventions in humans that aim to improve mental functioning beyond what is necessary to sustain or restore good health" (Dresler et al., 2019; Juengst, 1998). Dresler et al. (2019) discuss both pharmacological and non-pharmacological means of improving mental capabilities as part of enhancement and categorize multiple cognitive enhancing interventions under three main clusters: Biochemical, physical, and behavioral enhancement strategies.

Biochemical strategies include pharmacological enhancers such as synthetic stimulants such as amphetamine, methylphenidate (MPH), or antidementia drugs such as memantine; however, they are not limited to these pharmaceuticals. Dresler et al. (2019) include nutritional components such as caffeine, glucose, and flavonoids in cocoa, folic acid, and omega-3 fatty acids that have shown to enhance cognition under biochemical strategies.

Physical cognitive enhancement strategies range from various brain stimulation technologies such as electrical, magnetic, acoustic, or optical stimulation methods as well as other methods that target brain processes more indirectly such as whole-body vibrations, different forms of neurofeedback interventions that have the potential to improve memory and sustained attention (for details, please see Dresler et al., 2019). Most recently, augmented reality gadgets, wearable electronic memory aids, or more permanent bodily implants have been developed that converge mind and machines.

Finally, behavioral strategies that are not as commonly recognized as cognitive enhancers such as sleep, physical exercise as well as cultural activities, including musical training, dancing, or learning a second language, are shown to improve cognitive functioning (Bialystok et al., 2012; Coubard et al., 2011; Feld & Diekelmann, 2015; Schlaug et al., 2005). Interestingly, meditation training is considered among behavioral strategies from ancient times that have been developed to intentionally enhance certain cognitive processes such as attention processes and mindfulness (Chiesa et al., 2011; Sedlmeier et al., 2012).

Hildt (2013) explains that the term "enhancement" is distinct from "treatment," as it specifies methods or technologies that aim to improve human capacities and performance in *healthy* individuals. Based on this difference, the use of MPH like Ritalin in the treatment of attention deficit hyperactivity disorder (ADHD), for instance, would not be considered enhancement. The treatment-enhancement distinction might not always be straightforward and clear; however, it is crucial to explore the multifaceted strategies and technologies underlining their differences, side effects, and implications to have an informed debate on the heated and risky topic of cognitive enhancement and to avoid the trivialization of the technological forms of enhancement such as brain implants.

The trivialization of technological forms of enhancement takes place through the rhetoric of how humankind have always striven to improve themselves in various ways and how we have been:

> enhancing our brains through written language, printing, and the Internet.... And we are all aware of the abilities to enhance our brains with adequate exercise, nutrition, and sleep.... newer technologies such as brain stimulation and prosthetic brain chips, should be viewed in the same category as education, good health habits, and information technology...
>
> (Greely et al., 2008, p. 702)

Technological enhancements such as brain implants radically differ from the traditional strategies in terms of implications, risks, and ethical concerns. The general argument that humans have always sought to improve themselves trivializes the crucial discussions that need to take place regarding the risks, principles, and policies concerning the ethics of cognitive enhancement. As Jotterand (2008) along with McKenny (1997) state, exercising prudence is of utmost importance in making wise choices regarding the role of medicine and technology in our lives on the verge of a potential paradigm shift (further discussed below) that the new innovations in techno-science (such as BCI) bring.

Jotterand (2008) writes that interventions in the brain through BCI not only enhance but "possibly alter the human sensory and physical capabilities" (p. 18), and transform our understanding of human nature, raising crucial questions on agency, personhood, free will, the relation between body and mind, among other aspects of ourselves. Jotterand (2008) explains that BCI that focus on *therapy* (restoration) and *enhancement* (improving mental and biological capacities such as data processing, reasoning, remembering) are still within the boundaries of the biological world (species typical) and remain human in their nature. The next level of application of emerging technologies in neuro sciences, however, focuses on *alteration* of neurobiological functions, with the goal "to transcend biological boundaries through technological means to alter human capacities (species atypical)" (Jotterand, 2008, p. 17). Thus, at the level of alteration, there is a transgression of biological boundaries through technological means, which is an alarmingly controversial issue that we cannot afford to trivialize.

For instance, *neural alteration* involves adding new features to brain functions (BCI, brain-to-brain interfaces, web access, etc.) through implants, microchips, and other hardware. Implantable brain devices can monitor brain activity in real time and forecast specific neuronal events (Gilbert, 2015). A particular form of BCI can detect, map, and stimulate affective states (Steinert & Friedrich, 2020). Brain-to-brain interfacing (BTBI) allows direct transfer of information between two brains (Trimper et al., 2014). All of these emerging biotechnological cognitive enhancement strategies raise major ethical questions regarding privacy, autonomy, manipulation of mental and affective states, mental integrity, moral decision-making and responsibility, and potential for coercive control.

As Trimper et al. (2014, p. 3) clearly underline, ethical discourse "must keep pace with the advances in technology" and "ethicists and scientists must work together to ensure that the technology is developed with the highest ethical standards." Yet, biomedical technologies, and specifically the neurotechnology of BCI, are fast growing and the focus on the moral implications and acceptability of BCI's (especially beyond therapeutic applications) enhancement and alteration of human neurological capacities as well as their regulation fall behind. A recent example from 2020 is illustrative: During the live question-and-answer session of the demonstration of a new brain implant by Neuralink, a neurotechnology company that envisions a future of symbiotic life with artificial intelligence, team members consisting of neuroscientists, engineers, programmers, chip designers, along with the cofounder of the company Elon Musk, received questions from the audience through Twitter. The questions and the discussion focused on the technical aspects of the brain chip, including device installation, speed, bandwidth, effective use, capabilities, and algorithms. There were no questions or concerns raised regarding the ethical, social, cultural, implications, acceptability, or potential future risks regarding the development and use of this product.

Furthermore, and even more concerning were some of the expressions of several Neuralink team members as they responded to questions from the audience regarding the brain implant: "a robot is a human's best friend" (CNET, 33:53), "the body is not a friendly place to be" (in reference to the implant), and "it's a very corrosive environment" ("it," referring to the brain, being corrosive for the electrodes that connect the chip to the brain). The objectification of the body as an "it" to be enhanced that is not a friendly habitat from the perspective of a brain chip implant, and the antihuman rhetoric that frames the human as less than a robot and deficient (as a friend or in terms of performance in general), are not only highly problematic and need to be scrutinized, but can also be dangerous in terms of our understanding of who we are as human beings, our place in the world in relation to others, and our well-being. As Rushkoff (2019) writes in *Team Human*:

> We are embedding some very old and disparaging notions about human beings and their place in the natural order into our future technological infrastructure. Engineers at our leading tech firms and universities tend to see human beings as the problem and technology as the solution.
>
> (p. 5)

The framing of human beings as the problem and technology as the solution might be the ultimate example of figure/ground reversals that were discussed in the introduction section of this chapter, and a highly problematic and provocative one as well that needs to be attended to with utmost prudence, wisdom, and critical thinking.

In the next section, I explore three articles that examine the effects of implantable brain devices on autonomy, mental privacy and integrity, and freedom of thought.

Autonomy, Freedom of Thought, and Mental Privacy

In "A Threat to Autonomy? The Intrusion of Predictive Brain Implants," Gilbert (2015) examines the effects of predictive and advisory implantable brain devices on a patient's feelings of autonomy following surgery. Gilbert (2015) questions whether overreliance on predictive and advisory brain technologies may threaten patients' autonomy. Autonomy in this context specifically focuses on decision-making and choice which "requires that an individual exercise control over her or his decision or choice" (Gilbert, 2015, p. 6). Novel invasive biomedical technologies such as implantable predictive and advisory brain devices "can be programmed to advise the implanted patient ahead of time of oncoming symptoms or to automatically discharge a therapeutic response" (Gilbert, 2015, pp. 4–5). The advisory function of these brain implants "refers to the device's capacity to inform in advance a patient how she or he should act in order to avoid specific neuronal events; to some extent, these functionalities provide prescriptive measures to be undertaken" (p. 5). Thus, the question on the autonomy of individuals with an implanted device involves the degree of control and freedom in decision-making under the influence of predictive and advisory implants.

Based on a semi-structured interview with a patient who volunteered to be implanted with the first experimental advisory brain device capable of predicting epilepsy seizure, Gilbert's (2015) preliminary observations indicate that "the advisory functionalities increased his sense of autonomy by helping to reduce the uncertainty of having a seizure at any time with little or no warning" (p. 7). However, Gilbert (2015) underlines an important point to keep in mind regarding the paradox of predictive and advisory brain implants; they provide an increased degree of control to patients, yet "it is not clear whether, by extension, this may not diminish patient autonomy in some respects: in particular by increasing the degree of control *on* patients" (p. 7). As Gilbert (2015) explains, the (over)reliance on the device to permanently monitor, inform, and advice might lead a patient to develop a false sense of security and not consider the risk of signal failure, or reading error, or other possible dysfunctions that might increase the risk of harm (of taking too much or not enough medication). Furthermore, the patient may expect that the device always accurately advices what is going to or not going to happen rather than keep in mind that the advisory brain devices use and present electroencephalography (EEG) data as advice rather than the data itself. Feeling more confident, secure, and at ease due to sustained brain monitoring, patients might feel encouraged to act in ways they would not without the implant (Gilbert, 2015). Overall, Gilbert (2015) cautions that:

> this overreliance on advisory brain devices may generate decisional vulnerability for patients, which might threaten their capacities to make freely informed decisions on whether and how to proceed with advice received. Under the sustained influence of the device, a patient may lack decisional sovereignty. Where patients' decisional capacities are strongly influenced by advisory brain devices, they may become passive and less active in their acceptance of the advice received.
>
> (p. 8)

Despite the benefits and the potential that the predictive and advisory devices offer to patients, it is crucial to acknowledge and understand the unintentional and unexpected implications of these brain technologies and the potential harm that these medical monitoring neurotechnologies can cause. The next generation of predictive and advisory brain implants will be capable of administering therapeutic response such as delivering a drug or electric stimulation. These *automated* predictive devices will have the capacity to operate without needing to consult with the patient and get their consent before each treatment. This raises further ethical concerns regarding informed consent, patients' right to change or disengage the automatic setting, patients' sense of autonomy, and their sense of connection to their body and potential risks of estrangement, objectification, and disconnection.

In "Wired emotions: Ethical Issues of Affective Brain–Computer Interfaces," Steinert and Friedrich (2020) discuss the ethical issues regarding a recently emerging form of BCI "that is able to detect, influence and stimulate affective states" (p. 351). Affective states include emotions and moods. "An affective BCI is a system that uses neurophysiological signals to extract features that are related to affective states" (Steinert & Friedrich, 2020, p. 352). There are invasive (electrodes placed on the surface of the brain) and noninvasive (outside the head) technologies to measure brain signals. Affective BCI can be used to move people from one particular emotional state to another (Daly et al., 2016; Ehrlich et al., 2017). In therapeutic applications, affective BCI technologies can be helpful for people with emotional disorders or for people who experienced trauma (Steinert & Friedrich, 2020).

Collecting data about affective states of people, which is a very personal and sensitive domain, is an extremely controversial issue that raises major questions about mental privacy, security, informed consent, and autonomy. The use of affective BCI's to monitor and influence affective states involve the same ethical concerns regarding mental privacy that Mecacci and Haselager (2017) examined in their article on "brain reading" technologies that facilitate "the observation of brain structure and/or activity aimed at obtaining insights about mental states" (p. 444). While both affective BCI's and brain reading technologies can be beneficial in clinical and medical contexts, they indeed "generate a number of ethical concerns, from the potential use and abuse of collected personal data (Ienca & Haselager 2016) to Orwellian scenarios where peoples' liberties are at stake and minds can be coercively or covertly monitored" (Federspiel 2007; Mecacci & Haselager, 2017, p. 445). Despite the technical challenges and limitations of brain reading technology that is still in the early phases of development, it is crucial to have discussions and debate on potential implications and ethical challenges of this technology to promote societal awareness as well as to guide or even pause or stop its development.

Along these lines, Lavazza (2018) argues that the development of the latest neuroscientific technologies and devices has increased the possibility of risking mental/brain privacy and integrity in an unprecedented way. Mental integrity "is the individual's mastery of his mental states and his brain data so that, without his consent, no one can read, spread, or alter such states and data in order to condition the individual in any way" (Lavazza, 2018, p. 4). Mental integrity, as Lavazza (2018) proposes, includes both the issue of privacy and cognitive freedom, and "it is the first and fundamental freedom that an individual must be granted in order to have all the other freedoms considered relevant" (p. 4). Lavazza (2018) highlights mental integrity as the basis of freedom of thought, which includes the right and freedom to control one's own consciousness and thought processes. Lavazza (2018) proposes a technical principle for the protection of mental integrity: "Specifically, new neural prostheses should (a) incorporate systems that can find and signal the unauthorized detection, alteration, and diffusion of brain data; (b) be able to stop any unauthorized detection, alteration, and diffusion of brain data" (5). These principles offer important reference points for academic and public discussions that need to take place along with the development of new neural technologies.

Enhanced Yet Outdated Humans: A Constant Need for Updates?

Adding to the discussion of ethical issues and the implications of neurotechnological developments focusing on human enhancement, Sparrow (2015) cautions about the risk of obsolescence associated with the rapid and continuous improvement in human enhancement technologies. Assuming that technologies of human enhancement might improve somewhat close to the pace of contemporary consumer electronics (e.g. cellular phones or computers), Sparrow (2015) argues that in five years, the state-of-the-art enhancement will start to become outdated and in ten years it might become useless due to the infrastructure needed to maintain it:

> What if it is not our cameras and computers, but our bodies and our brains, that quickly become out of date and then effectively obsolete? What if we knew that, while enhancement would allow us to improve our own capacities, people born just a few years after us would have powers that put ours to shame?
>
> (Sparrow, 2015, p. 232)

As a result, each group of enhanced individuals might find themselves at the risk of being outcompeted by the next and improved group, resulting in an "enhanced rat race" (Sparrow, 2015, p. 232). Some might argue that people can simply update the enhancements;

however, with some forms of enhancements that are invasive (that require surgery) such as the brain implants, updates might be very difficult, dangerous, or not possible. And, what about the cost of new updates? What happens when some people are not able to afford the next update?

The idea that one's brain and body might become obsolete in a world of enhanced humans sounds daunting. It is the perfect scenario for objectifying the body and alienating people from their (outdated) bodies. The need for updates that one would need to keep up with to stay relevant and useful adds another layer that further complicates this disturbing issue. Sparrow (2015) writes about the kind of social order that would result from the pursuit of enhancement:

> If our enhancements will become obsolete, then even with the benefit of enhancement, people will spend most of their lives with substantially inferior capacities to an ever-growing proportion of the population. Once our enhancements are more than a few years old, younger people will have greatly superior powers to our own... Of course, as we become obsolete, those who secured their enhancements earlier than us will be becoming more so.
>
> (p. 239)

In this "enhanced rat race" that Sparrow vividly describes, competition, inequality, and anxieties that already exist in contemporary capitalist societies will also be enhanced. Following a detailed examination of multiple concerns regarding the enhanced rat race, including implications for children, Sparrow (2015) concludes that it would be rational to reject enhancements that initially might *appear* to be exciting yet worsen our circumstances and well-being.

Along with Sparrow's (2015) assertion that questions the implications of enhancements in terms of well-being and conditions of our coexistence, Earp et al. (2014) challenge the functional-augmentative approach to enhancement that focus on the *augmentation* of certain capacities such as learning, memory, attention, and so on. As an alternative, Earp et al. (2014) propose the welfarist approach to enhancement that underlines an understanding of enhancement in terms of "any change in the biology or psychology of a person which increases the chances of leading a good life in a given set of circumstances" (p. 2). Furthermore, Earp et al. (2014) introduce the notion of *diminishment as enhancement* in contrast to augmentation that highlights interventions that *weaken* certain capacities or functions that might contribute to individual welfare and realization of a good life. The welfarist approach to enhancement challenges the assumption that more is always better, such as enhanced recollection or concentration. Some examples that Earp et al. (2014) include are the *diminishment of recall* regarding wartime memories of soldiers or the *weakening* of the emotional attachment of a battered spouse with her abuser, *as enhancement*:

> Sometimes, diminishment *is* enhancement... once we shift our focus from the particular *capacity* or *function* being modified to the overall *normative goal* of the modification itself, we begin to see that 'enhancement' may be more broadly understood as having something to do with well-being—a goal that the welfarist definition makes explicit.
>
> (Earp et al., 2014, p. 4)

This discussion expands the understanding of "enhancement" beyond a particular function's augmentation to consider its implications on the whole system, thus reintroducing the part-whole/figure-ground framework to the debate that was underlined in the introduction of this chapter. The welfarist approach highlights that if the intervention increases the individual's overall well-being (rather than particular functions) and the chances of leading a good life, then it should be considered an enhancement.

Earp et al. (2014) do not engage in a discussion of what constitutes "good life" and/or "well-being," and they do not offer connections and implications regarding collective life and collective well-being beyond the individual as part of their welfarist approach to the debate on enhancement; however, their main point is clear: To distinguish functional enhancement that is framed with an emphasis on augmentation from enhancement of well-being. This is a crucial point and criteria to maintain at the center of any discussions on human enhancement, which ordinarily focus on parts (augmentation of a particular function) rather than the whole and present enhancement as a desirable, attractive, and even necessary choice without question. Savulescu et al. (2011) underline the connection between enhancement of individual well-being which might not be beneficial for the larger society due to its implications leading to greater injustice. It is not only essential to consider the part and the whole at the individual level as part of the human enhancement debates, but also the enhancement of the individual as connected to the larger collective contexts that they are embedded in and its consequences for others.

At the Crossroads: The (Post)Digital Age and Urgency for Thoughtfulness

In *A Human Algorithm: How Artificial Intelligence is Redefining Who We Are*, Coleman (2019) states that we are transitioning to a new age, which he refers to as the "Intelligent Machine Age" (p. xiii). "We are living at the end of the last cycle of technological development led entirely by humans" (Coleman, 2019, p. xv). Coleman (2019) cautions that as our lives become more and more enmeshed with computers and machines, we delegate more decision-making and problem-solving to them, using human memory less, handing over personal information, without acknowledging how much power we are giving to the algorithms that, in turn, predict and guide our decisions and behavior. As machines are developed to learn on their own through artificial intelligence algorithms without having to be reprogrammed by humans, they will also learn and act without human control. This raises a whole host of concerns and threat for the future of human life, yet the main focus of research and debate remains on the advancement of technology rather than its implications on humanity.

Along these lines, Maggi Savin-Baden (2021) highlights concerns and ethical issues that emerge in relation to the "postdigital future" and "the development and use of postdigital humans" (p. xv):

> The idea of a postdigital human in the 2020s suggests a different understanding of what it means to be human but also reflects the idea of 'post' as a critical stance towards the whole idea of being human in a digital age. We are in a world in which we are, as Virilio (1997) predicted, universally telepresent without moving our physical bodies. Thus, there is often a sense that we arrive and depart from spaces and encounters without actually doing so.

The postdigital human can maintain an absent presence, or a disembodied presence, across various spaces—if one can refer to this mode as presence. The postdigital interrupts conventional boundaries and understandings of relationality, embodiment, and responsibility towards the other. It is an emerging concept that involves multiple layers including questions around what it means to be human, human-machine interactions, artificial intelligence, enhancement of humans, mortality/immortality, robotics and robotics ethics, among many others.

Yet, even without speculating into the future, it is not difficult to simply observe the ways in which smartphones have been influencing and shaping many people's lives, creating an illusion of being connected but functioning effectively as technologies of disconnection and isolation that feed depression and anxiety. Yet, most people continue to participate in the "media environment" (Rushkoff, 2019, p. 81) that the smartphone creates by conforming to its influences. Rushkoff (2019) refers to a media environment as including the:

> behavior, landscape, metaphors, and values that are engendered by a particular medium… For example, a smartphone is more than just that device in our pocket. Along with all other smartphones, it creates an environment: a world where anyone can reach us at any time, where people walk down public sidewalks in private bubbles, and where our movements are tracked by GPS and stored in marketing and government databases for future analysis. These environmental factors, in turn, promote particular states of mind, such as paranoia about being tracked, a constant state of distraction, and fear of missing out.

> (p. 82)

Clearly, technologies that human beings design and create, in turn, design and create not only the external conditions in which people exist in but shape priorities, rhythms, values, and states of mind. Recognizing the ways in which certain media captivate our attention, shape human interaction, and stir the heart is crucial in making wise choices regarding how one guides one's life (individually and collectively) rather than surrendering one's autonomy to the dominance of a media environment. However, when people get captivated in a media environment due to entertainment, stimulation, addiction, or certain fears or desires, the capacity for this discernment diminishes.

The next section argues that the diminishment of the capacity to discern the impact of a techno-scientific innovation (including the enhancement technologies discussed earlier) and lack of necessary action to oppose its harmful implications on humanity individually and socially breeds "thoughtlessness," as Arendt (1963) described and cautioned against.

Resisting Thoughtlessness: Reduction of Humans to Information Processors and Communication to Information Processing

In *The Human Condition*, Arendt (1958) writes about the reaction to the launch of Sputnik in 1957, the earth's first artificial satellite, which expressed a sense of "relief about the first 'step towards escape from men's imprisonment to the earth'" (p. 1). Arendt (1958) critiques this commonplace reaction that ignores the gift of the earth which "may be unique in the universe in providing human beings with a habitat in which they can move and breathe without effort and without artifice" (p. 2). She explains that this conception of the earth as a prison for human beings as a wish to escape the human condition also manifests in scientific endeavors that attempt to produce superior human beings and alter their size, shape, and function without thinking and speaking about how we wish to use scientific and technical knowledge:

> If it should turn out to be true that knowledge (in the modern sense of know-how) and thought have parted company for good, then we would indeed become the helpless slaves, not so much of our machines as of our know-how, *thoughtless creatures* at the mercy of every gadget which is technically possible, no matter how murderous it is.
>
> (Arendt, 1958, p. 3) (Italics added)

Arendt's caution from 63 years ago regarding the path human beings might be taking if scientific knowledge and thoughtfulness depart from each other seems to be the path we are walking now. The human enhancement debate is moving forward rapidly celebrating the wonders of augmentation of certain functions of human performance to the point of uploading a human brain to a computer and digital afterlife, without necessarily taking the need for a pause for critical reflection seriously.

We might start by asking, for instance, "Whose cognitive enhancement, for whom, and for what purposes?" Rather than automatically assume that cognitive enhancement is necessary, needed, or good, in meeting the challenges of an increasingly complex information society and that the natural limitations of human cognitive capacity need to be overcome and improved to meet these challenges, one might pause to question and inquire into the limitations, costs, and risks of an "increasingly complex information society" in the first place to avoid the figure/ground reversal (Rushkoff, 2019) that this chapter started with in the introduction. Who is serving whom? When do we draw the boundaries in an increasingly complex information society and discern what might be too costly for human flourishing and well-being? When do we question and resist the anti-human rhetoric that frames human beings as deficient and not as good as robots that can perform faster? Just because technology and science facilitate the next step towards further efficiency, speed, and productivity, do we *automatically* jump into the wagon of "progress" in a train that does not know how to stop itself to reflect and discern and be part of an "enhanced rat race" (Sparrow, 2015, p. 232) to be disregarded in a few years as obsolete?

Questions like the above, among many others, constitute a crucial step of discussion which seems to be avoided and skipped easily, and one finds herself in the midst of a debate on cognitive enhancement where the basic assumptions on the issue are already in place: Cognitive enhancement is the necessary next step in human evolution, it is unavoidable, human performance need to be improved, and natural limitations of human cognitive capacities need to be overcome. It might even already feel too late to be asking questions since the race has already started. How close is this line of thinking or lack of thinking to the example I offered earlier on the conception of the earth as a prison for human beings that needs to be escaped?

Maggi Savin-Baden (2021) reminds of the "gift of the interval" which is vital "in order to take a critical stance towards being the postdigital humans and to enable us to recognize the ways in which we are becoming enmeshed in our postdigital world" (p. 13). The capacity to be able to take intervals within the digital that we already are embedded in resists "thoughtlessness" (Arendt, 1958) and offers a crucial preventative measure before diving into anything new that becomes techno-scientifically possible. Such reflective, critical pause is essential in resisting the anti-human rhetoric that reduces human beings to processors in a complex information system where they would eventually become obsolete compared to computers. We need to realize before too late that "people are both central to the postdigital and key players in its formulation, interruptions, and (re)creation" (Maggi Savin-Baden, 2021, p. 4).

References

Arendt, H. (1958). *The human condition*. University of Chicago Press.

Arendt, H. (1963). *Eichmann in Jerusalem; a report on the banality of evil*. Viking Press.

Bialystok, E., Craik, F. I., & Luk, G. (2012). Bilingualism: Consequences for mind and brain. *Trends in Cognitive Science 16*, 240−250.

Chiesa, A., Calati, R., & Serretti, A. (2011). Does mindfulness training improve cognitive abilities? A systematic review of neuro- psychological findings. *Clinical Psychology Review 31*, 449−464.

CNET. (2020). *Watch Elon Musk's ENTIRE live Neuralink demonstration* [Video]. Retrieved from https://www.youtube.com/watch?v=iOWFXqT5MZ4.

Coleman, F. (2019). *A human algorithm: How artificial intelligence is redefining who we are.* Counterpoint.

Coubard, O. A., Duretz, S., Lefebvre, V., Lapalus, P., & Ferrufino, L. (2011). Practice of contemporary dance improves cognitive flexibility in aging. *Frontiers in Aging Neuroscience 3*, 1–12.

Daly, I., Williams, D., Kirke, A., Weaver, J., Malik, A., Hwang, F., et al. (2016). Affective brain–computer music interfacing. *Journal of Neural Engineering 13*(4). https://doi.org/10.1088/1741-2560/13/4/046022.

Dresler, M., Sandberg, A., Bublitz, C., Ohla, K., Trenado, C., Mroczko-Wąsowicz, A. et al. (2019). Hacking the brain: Dimensions of cognitive enhancement. *ACS Chemical Neuroscience 10*(3), 1137–1148. https://doi.org/10.1021/acschemneuro.8b00571

Earp, B. D., Sandberg, A., Kahane, G., & Savulescu, J. (2014). When is diminishment a form of enhancement? Rethinking the enhancement debate in biomedical ethics. *Frontiers in Systems Neuroscience 8*, 12. https://doi.org/10.3389/fnsys.2014.00012

Ehrlich, S., Guan, C., & Cheng, G. (2017). A closed-loop brain–Computer music interface for continuous affective interaction. In 2017 international conference on orange technologies (ICOT) (pp. 176–179). Presented at the 2017 international conference on orange technologies (ICOT), Singapore: IEEE. https://doi.org/10.1109/icot.2017.8336116

Federspiel, W. (2007). 1984 Arrives: Thought (crime), technology, and the constitution. *William & Mary Bill of Rights Journal 16*, 865–900.

Feld, G. B., & Diekelmann, S. (2015). Sleep smart-optimizing sleep for declarative learning and memory. *Frontiers in Psychology 6*, 622, 1–11.

Gilbert, F. (2015). A threat to autonomy? The intrusion of predictive brain implants. *AJOB Neuroscience 6*(4), 4–11. https://doi.org/10.1080/21507740.2015.1076087

Greely, H., Campbell, P., Sahakian, B., Harris, J., Kessler, R., Gazzaniga, M., & Farah, M. J. (2008). Towards responsible use of cognitive-enhancing drugs by the healthy. Retrieved from https://repository.upenn.edu/neuroethics_pubs/42

Hildt, E. (2013). Cognitive enhancement – A critical look at the recent debate. In Hildt E., & Franke A. (eds). *Cognitive enhancement. Trends in augmentation of human performance*, vol 1. Springer. https://doi.org/10.1007/978-94-007-6253-4_1

Ienca, M., & Haselager, P. (2016). Hacking the brain: Brain–computer interfacing technology and the ethics of neurosecurity. *Ethics and Information Technology 18*(2), 117–129. https://doi.org/10.1007/s10676-016-9398-9.

Jacob, N., Evans, R., & Scourfield, J. (2017). The influence of online images on self-harm: A qualitative study of young people aged 16–24. *Journal of Adolescence 60*, 140–147. https://doi.org/10.1016/j.adolescence.2017.08.001.

Jotterand, F. (2008). Beyond therapy and enhancement: The alteration of human nature. *NanoEthics 2*(1), 15–23.

Juengst, E. T. (1998). What does enhancement mean? In Parens, Erik (ed). *Enhancing human traits: Ethical and social implications.* Georgetown University Press.

Keles, B., McCrae, N., & Grealish A. (2020). A systematic review: The influence of social media on depression, anxiety and psychological distress in adolescents, *International Journal of Adolescence and Youth 25*(1), 79–93. https://doi.org/10.1080/02673843.2019.1590851

Kross, E., Verduyn, P., Demiralp, E., Park, J., Lee, D. S., Lin, N., et al. (2013). Facebook use predicts declines in subjective well-being in young adults. *PLoS ONE 8*(8), e69841. https://doi.org/10.1371/journal.pone.0069841

Lanier, J. (2010). *You are not a gadget*. Vintage.

Lavazza, A. (2018). Freedom of thought and mental integrity: The moral requirements for any neural prosthesis. *Frontiers in Neuroscience 12*. https://doi.org/10.3389/fnins.2018.00082

Maggi Savin-Baden. (2021). *Postdigital humans: Transitions, transformations and transcendence*. Springer.

McKenny, G. P. (1997). *To relieve the human condition: Bioethics, technology, and the body*. State University of New York Press.

Mecacci, G., & Haselager, P. (2017). Identifying criteria for the evaluation of the implications of brain reading for mental privacy. *Science and Engineering Ethics 25*, 443–461. https://doi.org/10.1007/s11948-017-0003-3.

Ott, B. (2017). The age of Twitter: Donald J. Trump and the politics of debasement. *Critical Studies in Media Communication 34*(1), 59–68. https://doi.org/10.1080/15295036.2016.1266686

Rushkoff, D. (2019). *Team human*. W. W. Norton & Company.

Savulescu, J., Sandberg, A., & Kahane, G. (2011). Well-being and enhancement. In Savulescu, J., Meulen, R., and Kahane, G. (eds). *Enhancing human capacities*. Wiley-Blackwell, 3–18.

Schlaug, G., Norton, A., Overy, K., & Winner, E. (2005). Effects of music training on the child's brain and cognitive development. *Annals of the New York Academy of Sciences 1060*, 219–230.

Sedlmeier, P., Eberth, J., Schwarz, M., Zimmermann, D., Haarig, F., Jaeger, S., & Kunze, S. (2012). The psychological effects of meditation: a meta-analysis. *Psychology Bulletin 138*, 1139–1171.

Sparrow, R. (2015). Enhancement and obsolescence: Avoiding an "enhanced rat race". *Kennedy Institute of Ethics Journal 25*(3), 231–260.

Steinert, S., & Friedrich, O. (2020). Wired emotions: Ethical issues of affective brain–computer interfaces. *Science and Engineering Ethics 26*, 351–367. https://doi.org/10.1007/s11948-019-00087-2

Tobin, S., Vanman, E., Verreynne, M., & Saeri, A. (2015). Threats to belonging on Facebook: lurking and ostracism. *Social Influence 10*(1), 31–42. https://doi.org/10.1080/15534510.2014.893924

Trimper, J. B., Wolpe, P. R., & Rommelfanger, K. S. (2014). When "I" becomes "we": Ethical implications of emerging brain-to-brain interfacing technologies. *Frontiers in Neuroengineering 7*(4), 1–4, https://doi.org/10.3389/fneng.2014.00004

Twenge, J. M. (2019). More time on technology, less happiness? Associations between digital-media use and psychological well-being. *Current Directions in Psychological Science 28*(4), 372–379. https://doi.org/10.1177/0963721419838244

Virilio, P. (1997). *Open Sky*. United Kingdom: Verso.

Yee, N., Bailenson, J. N., & Ducheneaut, N. (2009). The proteus effect: Implications of transformed digital self-representation on online and offline behavior. *Communication Research 36*(2), 285–312. https://doi.org/10.1177/0093650208330254

3 Impersonal Computing
From Art School to Business Hub in Four Decades

Eleanor Dare

Introduction

In the late spring of 2021, the impact of UK government cuts to funding of university arts and humanities courses became vivid for those of us working within Higher Education (HE). Something akin to a metaphorical bloodbath of the arts and humanities is unfolding, with courses from archaeology to medieval history, critical business and French axed in a brutal response to a 50% decrease in state subsidy for non-Science, Technology, Engineering and Math (STEM) subjects. At the same time, universities such as Leicester and University of East London (UEL) appeared to make staff redundant based on their critical and political research as opposed to a failure of metricized performance. These devastating events are taking place within the context of an intensely neoliberal stage in education, work and culture, in which all aspects of life are modeled as forms of business. Neoliberalism is:

> the defining political economic paradigm of our time—it refers to the policies and processes whereby a relative handful of private interests are permitted to control as much as possible of social life in order to maximize their personal profit. Associated initially with Reagan and Thatcher, for the past two decades neoliberalism has been the dominant global political economic trend adopted by political parties of the center and much of the traditional left as well as the right. These parties and the policies they enact represent the immediate interests of extremely wealthy investors and less than one thousand large corporations.
>
> (Chomsky, 7, 1999)

The shift in focus for Art Schools within the Global North, from fine art to computer science and business studies, has been slow but steady

DOI: 10.4324/9781003173304-3

and arguably insidious, inculcating a neoliberal business ontology which seeks to neutralize the critical and indeed radical potential of non-positivist disciplines. It is clear that right-wing governments and ideologists are threatened by a perceived radicalism of the arts and humanities; since the *Entartete Kunst* ('Degenerate Art') exhibition of 1937, we should have no doubts as to the association of right-wing ideology with a distrust of non-propagandist and non-realist art with art which questions capitalist power structures, representation, production methods, social or sexual orthodoxies, neoliberal business ontologies and the will of Big Business to avoid taxes and regulation. Given that the arts and humanities contribute significantly to the UK economy (as mentioned in the UK government's own report into halving arts and humanities funding), it is obvious they represent something more to right-wing, neoliberal governments than employment implications. What such governments want to eradicate, it would seem, is any research or teaching which questions capitalism, including anti-racism and anti-colonialism, transgender and queer rights, climate emergency and regulatory research, anything which might challenge the entrepreneurial individualist ontology of unbridled capitalist growth, technological determinism and low taxes.

As evidence to the assertion above, this chapter draws upon the author's own career trajectory, from undergraduate study in UK art schools at the peak of Thatcherism and Reaganite economics, to being part of the Blair government's initiative to get more women into computing in the late 1990s, to the STEM and Science, Technology, Engineering, Arts and Math (STEAM) educational initiatives which sprang from the America Competes Act of 2007, the year the author began a funded PhD in Arts and Computational Technology at Goldsmiths, Department of Computing. This chapter analyses the current growth of Computing and Business centers within UK and more widely located Art and Design colleges, again drawing upon the author's later experiences of lecturing and senior management within STEM and STEAM disciplines. Analyzing the rise of STEM and STEAM via a critique of Design Thinking and managerialism, for whom technology represents an often tacit, sometimes explicit locus of wishful thinking. Some politicians similarly speak as if technology alone can resolve climate crises, conflicts with other countries, education and health, not to mention centuries of inequality and exploitation.

Key issues are summarized, and the author draws upon their own research and practice in the domain of computation and ideology, in particular the political imaginary projected onto the teaching of STEM and STEAM subjects within HE. This chapter aims to be of interest to those concerned with Science and Technology Studies, Digital Humanities, Communication Studies and pedagogy.

1968–1987, from School to University

In examining the context and chronology of my own educational background, I have come to understand the specific nuances of the educational indoctrination we are currently experiencing within the UK, in particular, the rise of managerialism, which is the subject of Fleming's book, *Dark Academia* (2021). Fleming writes:

> Impersonal and unforgiving management hierarchies have supplanted academic judgement, collegiality and professional common sense. In many institutions, senior executives have no PhDs and have been trained in business or the military instead. Mindless performance targets dominate teaching and research to the point of caricature, designed by functionaries who've never taught a class or written a research article in their lives. Unfortunately, these hierarchies have become notoriously bossy. Coercion rather than volition compels much academic labour today.
>
> (Fleming, 72, 2021)

In the UK and US, a growing army of administrators and business consultants increasingly define the activities and imperatives of HE. This was not always the case; an examination of my education confirms this shift in agency. I was educated within the British state school system, between the late 1960s and early 1980s, first in a coeducational ('boys' and 'girls') kindergarten, then in an affiliated primary school and after that what was then defined as a 'Comprehensive school for girls'. After I left school in 1983, I studied for one year at an art Foundation course, at a college formerly called Sir John Cass School of Art, which had evolved out of the Sir John Cass Technical Institute of 1902–1950. It is both important and relevant to the wider context of this paper to state that Sir John Cass was a slave trader. In 2020 the University removed his name from the college, which is now part of the London Metropolitan University called 'The School of Art, Architecture and Design'. The course was one of only a handful of Art Foundation courses which were officially recognized by the state, therefore enabling me to receive local authority funding in the form of a grant for living costs and full payment of fees.

After the Foundation course, I went straight into a degree course (also receiving a full grant) in Fine Art (Painting) at another London art school, the then independent Wimbledon School of Art, which was one of the last independent art schools in London, often promoting itself as 'London's only autonomous art school' (conveniently ignoring Byam Shaw school of Art which was also autonomous until it was taken over by Central Saint Martins College of Arts and Design in 2003). Wimbledon School of Art, like my Foundation college, had evolved from a technical institute, becoming an art school in 1930. In 1995, six years after I had graduated, Wimbledon School of Art issued degrees under the aegis of the University of Surrey, and in 1986 it joined the London Institute (the core of what later became UAL), by 2006 it was incorporated into the enormous University of the Arts (UAL), a 'federation' consisting of six colleges, and renamed Wimbledon College of Arts. My curriculum vitae (CV) is therefore a source of confusion, as, like Wimbledon, almost every college I have studied or worked at has been subject to rapidly shifting affiliations. The colleges I attended have been renamed, rebranded and reoriented from technical institutes to art schools, to art and design colleges, to creative computing institutes; their identities have been transmuted from schools of math and computing to business schools.

It was another ten years before I returned to education. I had always perceived my educational and working life as largely nonlinear, driven by and large by a series of apparently chance decisions and unplanned outcomes; however, researching and writing this chapter has changed my perception of that trajectory. Instead, it is now clear to me that a succession of epistemic and wider political power struggles within and between states has had a significant impact on my own educational trajectory.

My first paid teaching work entailed, from 2007 to 2017, lecturing on computer programming and broader computational processes for MA, BSc and MSc students at departments of computing and mathematics at Goldsmiths the Open University and the University of Derby Online. In middle age and beyond, I have taught topics latterly described as 'creative computing' at UAL and the Royal College of Art (RCA) as well as coordinating online learning and training for what were, pre-COVID, often reluctant lecturers at London College of Communication (LCC), which when I first studied Sound there was called London College of Printing. I was also head of an MA course about storytelling and emergent technologies at the RCA, one which was often presented as a STEM/STEAM course. Indeed, in 2017 I presented a paper about the course at a large Beijing STEM/STEAM conference, in which it became clear to me that STEM and STEAM are perceived as drivers of unlimited economic growth, including military expansion; this association of STEM and STEAM with military expansion is common to the US, UK, China and many other countries. It was the beginning of my critical relationship to the concept of STEM and STEAM. When I returned from that conference, I removed the words STEM and STEAM from my CV and LinkedIn profile.

As I write, I am now in my late 50s, old enough to have experienced schooling with no computers, for there were no such machines at my first school, other than abacuses and the *high-tech* visual imaginary of the 'space race'. At my secondary school (English children generally study in secondary schools from the age of 11 until they leave school at 16 or 18, though there are also Middle Schools in some areas of the UK for children aged 10–14), there was one computer, locked in a tiny room and accessible only to an elite of pupils studying A Level (Advanced level) Mathematics. At art school between 1983 and 1987 there were no computers, but in my final year, 1987, I wrote my dissertation on a new-fangled device, a small Brother word processor with a two-tone digital display which showed three or four words at once. At a cost of about £110, my Brother word processor was the most expensive item I had ever bought. Alas, it had no storage. I typed my dissertation on thermal paper, which has now faded completely. Though I was oblivious at the time to the ideological backdrop of my own education, Anft reminds us that:

> Before Americans were pulling their hair over threats from China and India to our pre-eminence as a global innovator, there were ruckuses caused by an increase in foreign auto and electronics imports (Japan) in the 1970s and 1980s, a fear that someone else (the U.S.S.R.) would win the space race in the 1950s and 1960s, and the wartime emergency (Nazi Germany) that led to the Manhattan Project in the 40.
>
> (Anft, 2013)

Furthermore:

> The pedestal placement of science and technology in the United States may go back even further. The federal Morrill Act of 1862 created land-grant colleges in most states and shifted the emphasis of higher education away from the study of classics and toward "real world" studies, including agriculture, home economics, and "the mechanical arts." Nowadays many of those same colleges, like Ohio State and Purdue University, boast large engineering schools.
>
> (Anft, 2013)

Following graduation from UK Art School with a degree in Painting in 1987, I proceeded to work at a low level in market research, restaurants and libraries against a backdrop of mass unemployment. Joblessness had reached its peak in the UK in 1984 at above three million unemployed, a rate of '11.9% of the UK population aged 16 and over were out of work' (Burkitt, 2020). Towards the end of the 1980s, and for the first time in my life, I began to work on a computer, as the market research firm I worked for proudly claimed to be one of the first in Britain with a computerized system, in which the phone numbers we rang were generated for us and we entered responses to surveys into a database. Despite earning my living via computer work, I still had no conception of myself as part of a digital economy, let alone a STEM or technology worker. My sense was that I was a fine artist, making a living on what we might now call a *side hustle* to my real job, largely unpaid, of painting. The libraries I worked in, in Inner London, did not have computers – they had microfiche and cardboard tags held in wooden cabinets. By the late 1990s, things were not going so well; local libraries were shut down, increasingly centralized into 'computer hubs', in which books were downgraded in favor of internet access and digital 'literacy'. With hindsight, the pattern is clear: transitioning state provision from libraries, universities, schools and further education as centers of lifelong (and qualitatively life enhancing) learning towards the idea that UK citizens must be ready to work within the burgeoning tech and service industries. Within HE, those priorities were also beginning to strongly emerge. Now, in 2021, the lack of state commitment to the arts and humanities, combined with an explicit sense that they are considered irrelevant, ill-matched to employer's needs, is enshrined in government policy. In the USA, in 2013, Republican governors:

> proposed cuts to humanities departments at state universities to rebalance funding towards more obviously "practical" subjects. North Carolina's governor, Patrick McCrory stated in January 2013, that he planned to change the state's legislation on higher education funding so that "it's not based on butts in seats but on how many of those butts can get jobs." Like other critics, McCrory did not want taxpayers to subsidize subjects that did not seem to lead directly to students securing a job.
>
> (Tworek, 2013)

In the UK, the Office for Students consultation document of 2021 states that there will be a 'reduction by half to the rate of high-cost subject funding for other price group C1 subjects – that is, for courses in performing and creative arts, media studies and archaeology' (Officeforstudents, 14, 2021), adding:

> In anticipation of this further increase in student numbers, we believe it right that we should increase the budget for high-cost subject funding beyond the £744 million. We therefore propose to increase the total high-cost subject funding to £756 million, but within this, to enhance further the rate of funding for STEM and healthcare disciplines and reduce the rate of funding for other subjects.
>
> (Officeforstudents, 17, 2021)

Confusingly, the document justifies cuts to the arts by asserting that there are 'shortage occupations' in STEM areas, but it then states:

> The list includes professionals working in many STEM subjects, but also includes archaeologists; artists; dancers and choreographers (only skilled classical ballet dancers or skilled contemporary dancers who meet the standard required by internationally recognised UK ballet or contemporary dance companies); musicians (only skilled orchestral musicians who are leaders, principals, sub-principals or numbered string positions, and who meet the standard required by internationally recognised UK orchestras); arts officers, producers and directors.
>
> (Officeforstudents, 18, 2021)

Which begs the question: who benefits from the convergence of education to STEM-themed subjects? While arts and humanities courses have been undermined by right-wing, neoliberal governments, there has been a simultaneous attack on the construct of a 'cancel culture', the largely fictitious idea that students are constantly censoring speech on campuses. In America, President Trump sought to ban anti-bias training which acknowledges systemic racism, issuing the following edict in 2020:

> All agencies are directed to begin to identify all contracts or other agency spending related to any training on 'critical race theory, ' 'white privilege, ' or any other training or propaganda effort that teaches or suggests either (1) that the United States is an inherently racist or evil country or (2) that any race or ethnicity is inherently racist or evil, it says.
>
> (whitehouse.gov, 2020)

It is clear we are witnessing an attempt to shift education (and indeed all wider institutions, including health and media) to a right-wing monoculture to dominate and indoctrinate students in what has become a sometimes hidden and at other times overt curriculum of right-wing ideology, converging upon corporations seeking epistemic control. LinkedIn, Pearson, Google, Edison Schools, among others, have clearly stated ambitions to dominate all levels of education. Twenty-One years ago, Monbiot warned us:

> Education management in Britain looks as if it is about to become big business. In February 1999, King's Manor School in Guildford, Surrey, became the first state school in Britain whose administration was handed over to a private company. One month later, the government announced that it would contract out educational services to private companies in Hackney, east London. In November 1999, the Department for Education and Employment named a consultancy company as its 'preferred bidder' to run the schools in the London Borough of Islington.
>
> (Monbiot, 4462, 2000)

Such corporations form a hidden curriculum, one in which authority tacitly embeds sets of values and beliefs by way of ordered and structural school procedures and routines (Aubrey, 140, 2017). This, I would argue, is part of the drive to replace the arts and humanities with STEM. This would also support the ambitions of Google, LinkedIn and Pearson limited (corporations with large educational interests) to take over all education. Critical Arts and Humanities are arguably irreconcilable with these corporations; it is hard to imagine a radical degree in Fine Art run by Pearson, Google or Facebook, especially those which critique corporate power and ethical compromises. In relation to Google Classroom, Perrotta et al. write:

> Following mass school closures resulting from the Covid-19 pandemic, by April 2020 the company reported 120 million users of G Suite across 250 countries and 54 languages; over 100 million active users of Classroom, doubling its reach from 50 million a month before; and a 60% share of the market in education computers in the US (De Vynck et al., 2020). While such statistics do not reveal whether or how Google has reshaped pedagogic participation, they do illustrate its increasing structural dominance over competitors.
>
> (Perrotta et al. 2020)

The recent dismissal of Google artificial intelligence (AI) experts, Timnit Gebru and Margaret Mitchell, for highlighting the ethical and environmental problems inherent in large-scale machine learning processes (Reuters, 2021) serves as a warning to us of the dangers of allowing Google and other corporations to define what education can be. Perrotta et al. describe Google's increasingly complex network of platforms in which:

> all those categorised as platform users (teachers and students) are involved in a laborious relationship with Google, as interactions deliver training data for its proprietary AI. In this sense, every click has the potential to deliver value, which is extracted by Google to refine its commercial productivity tools.
>
> (Perrotta et al. 2020)

It is significant that in the UK, Prime Minister Theresa May's Industrial Strategy was recently abandoned (March, 2021), replaced with a 'Growth Strategy' involving tax breaks for large investors, Freeports and the notorious prime ministerial advisor Dominic Cummings's Advanced Research and Invention Agency (ARIA). ARIA is supposedly modeled on 'the US' Defense Advanced Research Projects Agency (DARPA) for experimental military research. In 2021 Kelly wrote:

> Cummings is unconcerned that granting "extreme freedom" to ARIA could result in less transparency over who gets selected for funding. Labour MP Dawn Butler, who sits on the science committee, said ARIA's exemption from freedom of information requests would "raise alarm bells" about how taxpayers' money was being spent, given recent scandals about how contracts for emergency procurement of personal protective equipment were handled.
>
> (Kelly, 2021)

The idea that 'odd' people should run ARIA, as publicly stated by Cummings, seems to be a synonym for those without ethical limits, focused as it is on an AI-driven militarized model, supercharging a technology-driven 'cold war' with China. But it is also driven by a rejection of UK HE, with Cummings explicitly stating that ARIA should not put a 'bog standard vice chancellor' (Kelly, 2021) in charge. Cummings's evocation of a 'bog standard vice chancellor' cannot fail to suggest a sense of superiority towards HE, likening it to the infamous (within the UK) term, 'bog standard comprehensive'. The comment about 'bog standard' comprehensive schools was made by Labour

Prime Minister Tony Blair's advisor Alastair Campbell in 2001; the term 'bog standard' means common, it now has the connotation of maligning the educational standards and aspirations of working-class people, who are more likely to attend state schools in the UK.

Business and Technology Education Council

Fourteen years earlier, in 1997, the term 'bog standard comprehensive school' had not yet been used to disparage state schools or their products, such as myself, nor had the culture of huge wealth disparities between lecturers and vice chancellors yet been established or the widespread deployment of lecturers on precarious contracts. It was in a mood of enthusiasm that I entered another phase of my education, returning to college in 1997 to study something I had never heard of before, called a Business and Technology Education Council (BTEC) in Multimedia.

I was offered a place on a free 'BTEC' course at Carshalton College in1997, during another period of high unemployment in the UK. Carshalton is a small, further education college in the suburbs of South London. In retrospect, the creation of the 'Women into Multimedia' course is likely to have been influenced by a number of reports analyzing the role of women in a technologically driven economy, including Teresa Rees's report of 1992. Rees's report for the Commission of the European Communities addressed 'the domestic "brain drain" in high technology. The subject was women's underrepresentation in jobs created by new digital information technologies, especially in positions of power and responsibility' (Hicks, 361, 2017). The BTEC in Multimedia course was aimed at getting women ready for work within the growing area of digital media. At the time, Carshalton College reported that:

> The college runs courses which are specially designed for women in information technology, multi-media, and enterprise training. These courses have proved particularly helpful to women who have been made redundant or are retraining after bringing up their children.
>
> (FEFC, 4, 1997)

Though I was naively unaware of it at the time, these courses were entangled with the growing presence of marketing and public relations teams within UK Higher Educational institutions as well as a rise in service industries within the wider UK economy. Indeed, the college's annual report stated:

The public relations and communications team uses extensive market research and labour market information to inform its marketing and to provide a basis for changes in the range of courses which the college offers. 'Marketing focus groups' have been developed in each of the college's curriculum sectors and in the enterprise and training service, which is responsible for developing self-financing work (FEFC, 4, 1997) The college has made successful bids to a range of funding sources, including the European Social Fund and the funding resulting from these bids has enabled the college to provide a range of courses for large national companies in subjects such as customer service training and accountancy.

(FEFC, 4, 1997)

While this agenda was not immediately apparent to me within the course content, for the first time in my life I encountered the Internet, emailing, digital editing of sound, Photoshop and Illustrator, digital video cameras and film editing software. At that point, I had little sense of how I might use these systems and processes in 'the real world' or any sense that I would have access to it away from a college course. It was another five years before aspects of these systems became pervasive and their presence in my own life equally ubiquitous. Despite what was for me a hugely positive experience of staff who were hard working, knowledgeable and caring towards students, the Carshalton College report critically noted that not all students or staff were able or willing to adapt to new technologies and skills, stating:

> Although many students take up opportunities to improve their expertise with information technology, some are reluctant to use computers. In art courses, little use is made of computers. Few students on health and social care courses word process their work.
>
> (FEFC, 16, 1997)

There is a note of both disappointment and disapproval that the college's art courses, staff and students are not adapting to the use of Information Technology, signaling the beginning of another shift in the teleology of arts education, towards neoliberal instrumentalism and service to government and corporate technological agendas.

Neoliberal Choice in an Era of Technological Convergence

The idea of choice is a key component of neoliberal societies; neoliberalism is itself 'a pervasive and increasingly global ideology, associated with the favoring of free market competition and private property rights, reduction or abolishment of government intervention and expenditure, and valuation of individual "freedom of choice"' (Carlquist et al., 2014). My perception is increasingly that my own educational choices were foreclosed by a hidden curriculum of STEM and STEAM indoctrination, which is, in turn, a cover for neutering and privatizing education, converging power upon a few dominant corporations who seek to take over all aspects of education, from primary schools to universities. What were once Math and Computing departments are now increasingly subsumed into Business schools. Every college I have worked at now has growing business hubs, MBA courses and entrepreneurial units, while also measuring the value of research projects and academics by the number of patents they generate as well as a narrow construct of their business facing value. Such institutions are now heavily invested in concepts such as 'disruption' and 'agility', underpinned by Design Thinking and 'digital transformation' fuelled by a:

techno-determinist belief in reductionist, 'universal' (as in white Western) design 'solutions'. From a techno-determinist position there is no need to address systemic power disparities or colonialism – the presumption is that technology can find an answer for everything and everyone, apart from, of course, the so-called 'wicked problems' of poverty and inequality. Post-pandemic, neoliberal Design Thinking constructs risk becoming ever more entrenched within Higher Education, naturalised by the domination of STEM/STEAM agendas, with their racist assumptions of 'universal' values and needs.

(Dare, 2020)

Underpinning the manipulation of student's choices is the value judgment explicitly stated by the Information Technology & Innovation Foundation (ITIF):

The distribution of degrees right now is entirely up to students. Shouldn't we be steering them into degree types that are of more value to society, such as computer science or engineering? The American tradition is one of hard-core pragmatism. We're at risk of losing that, and we're in trouble now in regards to competitiveness.

(Charette, 2013)

The BTEC course at Carshalton was my first experience of business and digital technology in the context of an art's related processes such as drawing, sound recording, filmmaking and graphics, but over the next two and a half decades it would gain increasing dominance as the inevitable and correct trajectory for all Art education. Alas, and despite the apparently benign intentions of those who instigated initiatives to involve women in the 'information economy', as Hicks stated of earlier initiatives: 'lasting career gains were usually only possible for those who had uninterrupted careers and who were judged suitable for supervisory roles' (Hicks, 366, 2017). This chimes with my own experience and observation of both computing education and the labor divide within technology firms, confirmed by Hick's observation that:

> Even today, the US Census Bureau reports, for instance, that men with science, technology, engineering, and mathematics (STEM) degrees are twice as likely to be hired into STEM jobs as women with the same qualifications—ensuring that no matter how many women fill STEM pipelines problems with women's underrepresentation and undervaluation will continue. Contemporary situations like this become less surprising when one sees how the professional identity of computer workers is tied to a history of structural discrimination that has nothing to do with skill.\
> (Hicks, 366, 2017)

These outcomes are a reminder that technology does not and cannot exist outside of wider power relationships and historical inequalities; rather, it mirrors them in its own practices and its own visions. Analyzing the history of the several art schools, I have studied and taught at shows that what we are currently witnessing is not new, but rather, in many important ways, a reversion of art education to a Victorian industrial model. It is worth remembering that no less a college then the RCA always existed within the context of colonial and industrial ambitions:

> Like the Victoria and Albert Museum the Royal College of Art originated in the movement for popular education in industrial design of the 1830's. In 1837 a metropolitan School of Design was opened in Somerset House and by 1857, renamed the Normal Training School of Art, had removed under the auspices of the Science and Art Department to South Kensington, where it shared a site with the new museum.
> (Sheppard, 1975)

It is interesting to also note that despite Prince Albert's desire to have the Schools of Design renamed as 'Trade Schools', he was thwarted 'by a lack of enthusiasm for industrial designing on the part both of students and manufacturers' (Sheppard, 1975). Prince Albert's identification with technology and science is currently deployed by STEM advocates, as noted by *The Engineer*, reporting on a new initiative in which:

> The Great Exhibition at Home Challenge is very much in the spirit of Prince Albert's legacy. He would urge us to tackle the immediate challenges we face with the pandemic, but not to lose sight of the long-term goals. Prince Albert was a master of innovation and sought to promote it all his life, reminding us of the need to support and develop our young people and to nurture their curiosity. I am looking forward to seeing what young people today make of Albert's story and the ways in which it will inspire them to create new inventions for 2020 and beyond.
>
> (The Engineer, 2020)

The Victorian model of education is itself informed by medieval distinctions between the Liberal and Mechanical arts. Contemporary initiatives fuel a resurgence of what might be characterized as a corporate public pedagogy, entangled with what appears to be unquestionably benign constructs of STEM and STEAM. It is also now often connected to revisionist pedagogy, sadly enabled by the move to mass online learning. Throughout the pandemic, I have witnessed a reversion to a nineteenth-century pedagogy, with students often muted or not able to use cameras, neither seen or heard, or worse, a construction of 'flipped' learning deployed in such a way as to mask dogmatic, uncritically neoliberal technical teaching, focused on 'making' but without a systematic analysis of its contexts and trajectories, and serving instead a corporate agenda. The purpose of corporate public pedagogy is to:

> serve the individual in a competitive environment where material gain is to the fore. In the culture of corporate public pedagogy, matters of social injustice such as gender, race and social class issues are all undervalued and normalised for the sake of economic gain
>
> (Aubrey, 138–139, 2017)

STEM and STEAM ideology enforces the idea that those within the fine artists (as opposed to what were once defined as 'applied arts') should align with a technologically determinist and business outlook or face the idea that they have no relevance in a modern world. I do not agree with this assertion, but can see how pervasive it has become and how useful that assertion has been for right-wing governments in making huge cuts to the budget for the arts and humanities while asserting their own ideological imperatives.

America Competes, the UK Copies

Government programs to compete with other nation's technological advances, particularly China, included the America Competes Act of 2007, and in the UK, Theresa May's commitment to an 'AI revolution', which she stated would 'shape the world to come and will solve some of today's most pressing issues. Air pollution and congestion, quality healthcare, security and equal access to jobs are just a few examples of critical concerns we see in our cities and communities across the UK' (Poole et al., 2019). In 2015, the then President of America, Barack Obama, signed the 'Every Student Succeeds' Act. The law included 'mandates, and funding, to provide STEAM education in schools' (Catterall, 4, 2017). While the intention to increase the diversity of people engaging with science, technology, engineering and the arts (sometimes also incorporating the arts and humanities) is admirable in many ways, the outcome has arguably been divisive, redefining the arts as in service to the teaching of other, more corporate disciplines as opposed to nurturing the arts for the unique value it brings to our lives. STEM was driven:

> In part by the fear that the United States is falling behind in the STEM fields—government and private money is being poured into grants, scholarships, and job placement programs specifically tailored to STEM engagement and placing students in STEM careers in the U.S. (Some recent reports suggest that the ratio of STEM grads to STEM jobs is actually not a huge problem—there are other issues at play.).
>
> (Feldman, 2015)

STEM and STEAM, it seems, are predicated on what are largely unchallenged assertions about skills and workforce shortages. However, as Catterall states, there is no denying the lack of diversity within STEM within the US (and, I would add, the UK):

> If there was any part of the STEM conversation that rang true and continues to do so today, it's that there wasn't, and isn't, equitable opportunities to engage in STEM across our school systems. All students are not given equal opportunities to experience STEM subjects during their school years. Moreover, students who want

to pursue higher learning in STEM fields encounter deep institutional bias.

(Catterall, 1, 2017)

Of course, the notion of STEM and its various definitions also serves another purpose. It is used by immigration agencies generally to deny entry and freedom of movement. The 'U.S. Immigration and Customs Enforcement (ICE)agemcu uses a narrower definition that generally excludes social sciences and focuses on mathematics, chemistry, physics, computer and information sciences, and engineering' (Gonzalez et al., 2, 2012). The idea of employee and skills shortages are themselves open to question, with, as Anft states, most 'researchers who have looked into the issue—those who don't receive their money from technology companies or their private foundations, anyway—say no. They cite figures showing that the STEM-worker shortage is not only a meme but a myth' (Anft, 2013). Anft goes on to describe the close relationship between university management and the same organizations and corporations which promote the idea of skills shortages:

> Many of their institutions, of course, benefit from STEM-related partnerships with industries and federal STEM grants. Higher education receives about half of the total federal STEM education budget of $3.1-billion, according to the National Science and Technology Council. Colleges get grants from 14 agencies, including NASA and the National Science Foundation, to increase the number of STEM majors and grads, improve curricula, and bring more women and minority students into science and technology fields.
>
> (Anft, 2013)

Charette calls into question the existence of such skills shortages, stating 'there are more STEM workers than suitable jobs. One study found, for example, that wages for U.S. workers in computer and math fields have largely stagnated since 2000' (Charette, 2013). To question such shortages, in my experience, is to be met by shock, as if the construct is an unassailable orthodoxy, but as Charette states: 'at every stage of the career pipeline, from freshly minted grads to mid- and late-career PhDs, still struggle to find employment as many companies, including Boeing, IBM, and Symantec, continue to lay off thousands of STEM workers' (Charette, 2013).

The ITIF, 'an advocacy group that receives the bulk of its funding from tech companies', urges the federal government 'to widen the so-called STEM pipeline from school to work' (Anft, 2013). While STEM and STEAM initiatives are often presented as virtuously entangled with the aim of diversification and despite the efforts of Tony Blair's British Labour government (1997–2007) to change some aspects of the inequitable 'information economy' constitution, as Hicks writes:

> Today, despite decades of equal pay legislation and significant investment in educational strategies designed to change this situation on both sides of the Atlantic, patterns of underachievement and perceptions of women as less technically competent persist within Anglo-American culture, business, and higher education.
>
> (Hicks, 361, 2017)

Technological determinism, of course, fails to solve centuries-old problems of unequal power distribution, while STEAM arguably reduces the arts to a vehicle for promoting or even illustrating STEM. It was against this backdrop (which I now see as the idea of arts servicing STEM subjects) that I found myself the recipient of a generous doctoral studentship.

Impersonal Computing Teaching: A Personal History

In 2007, following completion of an MSc in Arts Computing at Goldsmiths, I obtained full funding from the Engineering and Physical Sciences Research Council (EPSRC), reputedly the first fine artist to do so. My PhD was in Arts and Computational Technology within the department of Computing at Goldsmiths, an institution with a reputation for edgy art practices and left-wing thought and action. I had not made a systemic analysis of the context of such an award at that point and presumed only that my own research had been deemed uniquely supportable. Yet, again, it did not occur to me that my own research fitted into a much wider political agenda, one which in many ways positioned STEM and STEAM as a defense against the talents of so many of the Chinese students who were paying our HE wages.

In return for the funding, I was apparently expected to teach one day a week. As accidental as it was, this was the beginning of my university teaching career, running a six-hour class on computer programming for predominantly arts educated masters students every Tuesday over two terms, something for which I was not at that point trained (not at all unusual in universities, I should add). I decided to base my pedagogy on a rejection of the way I had been taught while studying an MSc at Goldsmiths. During my MSc study, students from a range of largely non-computational backgrounds, such as fine arts, graphics and fashion, were required to sit in large lecture halls with BSc Computer Science students and listen to monologues about banking data bases and Java button widgets as well as attending data base structures and PostgreSQL 'laboratories' for this open-source, object-relational database system and Structured Query Language I had never heard of before.

While I found the subjects in some ways interesting, many students struggled to see their relevance or to grasp how and why they might deploy such learning in their own artistic practices. At no point was there any attempt to draw in philosophical, critical or political subjects or positions. We were taught only by male-identified lecturers. Eventually, one female-identified Arts Professor intervened to insist on teaching us a critical context, but it was clearly not part of the course design or validation document, which is not to critique the leader of that course rather the epistemic culture of computing departments in the early twenty-first century. The department's lack of diversity was not unique and reflected the underrepresentation found in many UK and US academies:

> only 17 percent were female at U.S. Ph.D.-granting computer science departments in 2009, and 22 percent were female at UK units in "computer software engineering" or "information technology and systems sciences" in 2004.6 Women are hired at top universities at a much lower rate than their representation in recent Ph.D.s, and they end up disproportionately concentrated in less prestigious community colleges and polytechnics or in insecure adjunct positions.
>
> (Abbate, 185, 2012)

Despite apparent shifts in ideology by changes in government, it is in many ways difficult to differentiate one administration from another; all of them appear to have been swayed by the idea of STEM skills shortages. All US and UK governments since Bush and Blair have made the same value judgment – STEM is superior to the arts, they are pressured by the same corporate interests and ideologies, the same technological determinism and imperative of maintaining, gaining or asserting digital industrial supremacy.

Conclusion

The US and the UK appear to rely evermore on the services of a few corporations for economic development and prosperity, for data and educational infrastructure, and this, in turn, is projected upon, among other key public services, housing and healthcare. In this context, it is truer than ever to say as Hicks does that the 'state and its priorities shape how technology is designed and used. Technology can support marginalized groups in the best cases, or it can participate in furthering their marginalization' (Hicks, 364–365, 2017). At the same time, HE is so deeply in thrall to all and any of the priorities and technologies promoted by such corporations, and seem, in my experience, almost incapable of critical distance from technological hyperbole. Even those who support such determinism warn of the privacy implications of increasing investment in data-driven services, as evidenced by the Horizon report of 2020:

> Higher education institutions continue to invest billions of dollars in analytics capabilities, and cost-benefit implications for student privacy will become an increasingly important consideration. Institutions will need to be more proactive in protecting student and employee data and must make careful decisions around partnerships and data exchanges with other organizations, vendors, and governments. Institutional relationships with technologies—and with platforms such as Facebook and Google—should reflect larger cultural preferences and tolerances for privacy.
>
> (Horizon Report, 2020)

With the emphasis on STEM as a curriculum priority comes the belief within HE senior management that reductionist analysis is the answer to all problems, with, as the Horizon Report states, billions of dollars invested in analytics and the data of student transactions becoming a commodity of such value it is the reason some businesses enter into education. Selwyn states: 'large-scale online educational systems are designed to maximize the analytic potential of their data usage' (Selwyn, 88, 2016). What seems like a virtuous project of widening participation in digital technology has apparently transmuted into something more sinister, closer to a project of educational indoctrination. Selwyn also reminds us that 'data are an ideal means of bringing market values and free market mechanisms into otherwise closed public education settings' (Selwyn, 92). Perrotta et al. remind us that corporate education is above all a process of extraction:

> It would be inaccurate to claim that the entirety of Google – an organisation employing over 100,000 people – is single-mindedly intent on the exploitation of personal data. However, in the dominant business models in the platform economy, a rhetoric of

openness and freedom-to-use conceals 'opacities that platform proprietors manage in their own interest' (Mackenzie, 5, 2019). Through these opacities, enabled by a sprawling apparatus of algorithms and specialist knowledge, digital platforms turn data into intangible assets, channelling them along financial circuits and subjecting them to capitalization.

(Perrotta et al. 2020)

After 14 years of teaching in HE and another 14 years as a student within the UK HE system, STEM and STEAM feel more and more like woefully deceptive constructs deployed to boost corporate domination and neoliberal ideology. I feel anxious for those being groomed for a life of neoliberal precarity and serfdom to the agendas of Google, IBM, Amazon and Facebook, often dressed up as a benignly inclusive future, when it is clearly the exact opposite. Despite the constant stream of STEM rhetoric, the UK government is not sincere in supporting the sciences. Indeed, funding for vital laboratories has been reduced:

Although the government's Integrated Review – published today – reaffirms its aim to secure the UK's position as a global science superpower, the announcement coincides with reports that the government is preparing to significantly cut the budget for research. This comes hard on the heels of a confirmed £120 million shortfall for research funded from the overseas development budget, which has forced universities across the country to abandon current research projects with international partners.

(Universities UK, March 2021)

What neoliberal governments mean by STEM and STEAM are in fact shallow business interests and fantasies of data-driven omniscience, as witnessed by the Test and Trace scandal in the UK during the COVID pandemic, in which:

it seems that the UK government is set to continue the scandal of commissioning Serco and other private companies to run the test and trace service. £37bn of taxpayers money is being given to this service—the figures are almost too large to comprehend.

(The BMJ Opinion, 2021)

The Cambridge Analytica scandal (2016) also points to the mixture of anti-democratic manipulation and wishful fantasy which neoliberal governments support. Trump's response to the pandemic is blatant evidence that the commitment to science and the push for a STEM agenda is insincere. STEM and STEAM as per the agenda of the America Competes Act, Trump's AI Task Force and UK government's endeavors since the 1990s are above all about neoliberalization, such that it prioritizes deregulation and the imperatives of a few dominant corporations and their putative 'skills shortages'. Who benefits from the withdrawal of funding for the arts and humanities or their conversion to buttresses for technology agendas? A better question might be: who suffers?

What I have learnt as an educator is that HE is a key arena for the social reproduction of inequality. In the last four decades, education has been marketized and students turned into customers, yet their rights and those of HE staff have diminished year on year. The impact of market ideology on universities has been profound, unsettling and ultimately destructive. I have witnessed the transition of universities from places engaged with critical academic imperatives (which I would still not seek to idealize) to sites of marketization and a projection of entrepreneurial ideology on all aspects of learning, with, from top to down, a depressing absence of criticality and a drift towards platitudes about innovation and business which serve the priorities of successive right-wing, anti-intellectual governments. As the COVID pandemic has shown us, such technological determinism and faith in unbridled capitalism has had a negative impact on equality and on the climate crisis, on poverty and health, let alone social mobility in education (Campos-Matos et al., 2020). The UK has experienced some of the worst COVID death rates in the world as well as growing child poverty and inequality. It is within this context that I find my values so starkly at odds with the trajectory of current HE.

The marketization of universities pulls academics apart, 'with the competing demands of their non-academic overlords and the newly powerful "consumers" of their "product" – the students' (Preston, 2015). It is in this framework, markedly intense within the UK, in which neoliberalism has overseen what risks being the destruction of the arts and humanities, 'creating the cumbersome research excellence framework (Ref), which seeks to audit the academics' research "outputs" and overseeing a dramatic increase in the number of staff on short-term contracts' (Preston, 2015). This is at odds with my own professional values. STEAM arguably reduces the arts to a vehicle for promoting or even just illustrating STEM ideas and processes, leaving us with the question I urge all colleagues and students to ask themselves: who really benefits from the convergence of education to

STEM-themed subjects and what do both the sciences and arts lose from the shallow focus on patents and business and the needs of a few unimaginably wealthy corporations?

References

Abbate, Janet (2012) *Recoding Gender* (History of Computing), Cambridge, MA: MIT Press. Kindle Edition.

Anft, M. (2013) 'The STEM crisis: Reality or myth?' *The Chronicle of Higher Education*, November 11, available at: https://www.chronicle.com/article/the-stem-crisis-reality-or-myth/

Aubrey, Karl (2017) *Understanding and Using Challenging Educational Theories*, Los Angeles/London/New Delhi/Singapore/Washington, DC/Melbourne: SAGE Publications, Kindle Edition.

The BMJ Opinion (2021) 'Covid-19 test and trace scandal—It's not too late to change the story', *blogs.bmj*, available at: https://blogs.bmj.com/bmj/2021/03/19/covid-19-test-and-trace-scandal-its-not-too-late-to-change-the-story/

Brown, M., McCormack, M., Reeves, J., Brook, D.C., Grajek, S., Alexander, B., Bali, M., Bulger, S., Dark, S., Engelbert, N., Gannon, K., Gauthier, A., Gibson, D., Gibson, R., Lundin, B., Veletsianos, G. & Weber, N. (2020) 2020 Educause *Horizon Report Teaching and Learning Edition*. Louisville, CO: EDUCAUSE.

Burkitt, S. (2020) 'Unemployment in the 1980s: 'It felt like a bereavement, I didn't know what was going on', 1st November 2020, *walesonline*, available at: https://www.walesonline.co.uk/news/wales-news/unemployment-1980s-it-felt-like-19149970

Campos-Matos, I., Newton, J., Doyle, Y. (2020) 'An opportunity to address inequalities: learning from the first months of the COVID-19 pandemic', Public health matters, available at: https://publichealthmatters.blog.gov.uk/2020/10/29/an-opportunity-to-address-inequalities-learning-from-the-first-months-of-the-covid-19-pandemic/ 29th October, 2020.

Carlquist, E., Phelps J. (2014) Neoliberalism. In: Teo T. (eds) *Encyclopedia of Critical Psychology*. Springer, New York, NY, available at: https://link.springer.com/referenceworkentry/10.1007%2F978-1-4614-5583-7_390#howtocite

Catterall, Lisa G. (2017) 'A brief history of STEM and STEAM from an inadvertent insider,' *The STEAM Journal*, 3(1), Article 5, available at: http://scholarship.claremont.edu/steam/vol3/iss1/5

Charette, Robert (2013) 'Is it fair to steer students into STEM disciplines facing a glut of workers?' IEEE Spectrum, available at https://spectrum.ieee.org/riskfactor/at-work/tech-careers/stem-crisis-as-myth-gets-yet-another-workout

Chomsky, Noam (1999) *Profit Over People*, Seven Stories Press. Kindle Edition.

Dare, Eleanor (2020) 'Teaching Machines: Platforms, pedagogies and the wicked problem of design thinking', *The Post-Pandemic University* [online], available at: https://postpandemicuniversity.net/2020/07/29/teaching-machines-platforms-pedagogies-and-the-wicked-problem-of-design-thinking/

The Engineer (2020) 'Engineering groups launch Great Exhibition STEM challenge for locked down pupils', *The Engineer*, available at: https://www.theengineer.co.uk/great-exhibition-stem-challenge/ 25th March, 2020.

FEFC (1997) 'Carshalton College. Report from the Inspectorate', *FEFC* (Further Education Funding Council).

Feldman, Anna (2015) 'STEAM rising why we need to put the arts into STEM education', slate.com, available at: https://slate.com/technology/2015/06/steam-vs-stem-why-we-need-to-put-the-arts-into-stem-education.html

Fleming, Peter (2021) *Dark Academia, How Universities Die*, London: Pluto Press, Kindle edition.

Gonzalez, H.B., Kuenzi, J.J. (2012) 'Science, technology, engineering, and mathematics (STEM) education: A primer', everycrsreport.com, available at: https://www.everycrsreport.com/reports/R42642.html

Hall, G. (2016) *The Uberfication of the University*, Minnesota: University of Minnesota Press.

Hicks, Marie (2017) *Programmed Inequality*, Cambridge, MA: MIT Press.

Kelly, Éanna (2021) 'Don't put a 'bog standard vice chancellor' in charge of new UK research agency', *Science Business*, available at: https://sciencebusiness.net/news/dont-put-bog-standard-vice-chancellor-charge-new-uk-research-agency

Monbiot, G. (2000) *Captive State: The Corporate Takeover of Britain*, London: Pan Macmillan. Kindle Edition.

Officeforstudents (2021) 'Consultation on recurrent funding for 2021–22', *Office for Students*, available at: https://www.officeforstudents.org.uk/media/8610a7a4-0ae3-47d3-9129-f234e086c43c/consultation-on-funding-for-ay2021-22-finalforweb.pdf

Perrotta, C., Gulson, K. N., Williamson, B. & Witzenberger, K. (2020) 'Automation, APIs and the distributed labour of platform pedagogies in Google Classroom', *Critical Studies in Education*, 62:1, 97–113.

Poole, G., Roughan, A. (2019) 'May's latest commitments to tech are welcome, but the next PM has more work to do', *Tech Newstatesman*, available at: https://tech.newstatesman.com/business/theresa-may-uk-tech 10th June, 2019.

Preston, Alex (2015) 'The war against humanities at Britain's universities', *The Guardian*, available at: https://www.theguardian.com/education/2015/mar/29/war-against-humanities-at-britains-universities accessed 29/01/2021

Reuters (2021) 'Google to change research process after uproar over scientists' firing', *The Guardian*, 26th February, 2021.

Selwyn, N. (2016) *Is Technology Good for Education?* Cambridge: Polity.

Sheppard, F. H. W. (1975) 'Royal College of Art'. In: Sheppard, F. H. W. (ed.) *Survey of London: Volume 38, South Kensington Museums Area*.

(London, 1975), pp. 260–261. *British History Online*, available at: http://www.british-history.ac.uk/survey-london/vol38/pp260-261 [accessed 4 June 2021].

Tworek, Heidi (2013) 'The real reason the humanities are 'in crisis', *The Atlantic*, available at: https://www.theatlantic.com/education/archive/2013/12/the-real-reason-the-humanities-are-in-crisis/282441/

Universities UK (2021) 'Government must urgently reconsider research budget cuts', *Universities UK*, available at: https://www.universitiesuk.ac.uk/news/Pages/govt-must-urgently-reconsider-research-budget-cuts.aspx

whitehouse.gov (2020) 'Memorandum for the heads of executive departments and agencies' *whitehouse.gov*, available at: https://www.whitehouse.gov/wp-content/uploads/2020/09/M-20-34.pdf

4 The *Plandemic* and Its Apostles

Conspiracy Theories in Pandemic Mode

Raúl Rodríguez-Ferrándiz

Introduction

Conspiranoia (conspiracy + paranoia) is a portmanteau term in the Spanish language which refers to that unhealthy propensity to see conspiracies where there are none. While both paranoia and conspiracy presuppose sinister intentions in others, there are a couple of striking differences: the first is an *imaginary* plot of the whole world against you, the second is an *authentic* plot of a small group against all or a significant part of society (Imhoff & Lamberti, 2018). Therefore *conspiranoia* is a strange word, because one of the ingredients contradicts the other: an imaginary, erroneous, false conspiracy. It is a term which is not registered in the most important English dictionaries, although the Urban Dictionary includes the word *conspiranoid*.[1]

In English the term for imaginary conspiracies is *Conspiracy Theories* (CTs, hereinafter), as we know. This is undoubtedly more benevolent than in Spanish, because these theories, although very bizarre, could eventually be confirmed, while *conspiranoia* is already described as an absurd manifesto. In any case, the idea of mixing conspiracy and paranoia came from an American sociologist Richard Hofstadter (1996 [1964]), who spoke specifically of the 'paranoid style' in American politics of the Cold War, an idea that was taken up by Kelly (1995), Pipes (1997), Fenster (2008, rev. ed.), Imhoff and Lamberti (2018) and Hellinger (2019). There has also been talk, in reference especially to American society, of a 'culture of conspiracy' (Goldberg, 2001; Knight, 2000), of an 'age of conspiracy' (Alter, 1997), and it has even been pointed out that we have entered a 'golden age' of conspiracy, particularly after 9/11, and that the web is an incredible accelerator of conspiracy plots (Fenster, 2008, rev. ed.). The tradition of conspiracy as an explanatory theory of society seems to have been exacerbated even more in recent years, particularly during the Trump administration (Hellinger, 2019;

DOI: 10.4324/9781003173304-4

Stanton, 2020). Swami et al. (2014) define CTs as 'false beliefs in which the ultimate cause of an event is due to a plot by multiple actors working together with a clear goal in mind, often lawfully and in secret' (2014: 572). And Cass R. Sunstein defines it as 'an effort to explain an event or practice by referring to the secret machinations of powerful people who have also managed to conceal their role' (2014: 35). For his part, Aaronovich (2009) states that a CT is the 'attribution of deliberate agency to something that is more likely to be accidental or unintended'. He believes that a 'conspiracy theory is the unnecessary assumption of conspiracy when other explanations are more likely'. And Basham (2006) explains that CTs follow a two-step pattern: 'first, they undermine official accounts via striking incongruities, next, they offer plausible but conspiratorial accounts that incorporate the incongruities into a framework where these then become wholly congruent'.

Karl Popper offered an explanation of what he called 'Conspiracy Theory of Society' as a secularization of theism, of the belief in gods whose whims and desires govern everything that happens (Popper, 2002: 165):

> Homer conceived the power of the gods in such a way that whatever happened on the plain before Troy was only a reflection of the various conspiracies on Olympus. The conspiracy theory of society is just a version of this theism, of a belief in gods whose whims and wills rule everything. It comes from abandoning God and then asking: 'Who is in his place?' His place is then filled by various powerful men and groups—sinister pressure groups, who are to be blamed for having planned the great depression and all the evils from which we suffer.

In a way, CTs are mythologies of modernity: they do not resort to supernatural beings, such as Zeus, Athena or Poseidon, but they assume that certain events of historical, political and social scope are due to a plan conceived in secret by a small group of very powerful entities: Freemasons, Jesuits, Witches, Jacobins, Jews, Illuminati, Bilderberg Club, Federal Government, aliens, UN, UNESCO, Rothschilds, Rockefellers, Bill Gates, George Soros, WHO.

Conspiracy Theories' Rhetoric: Tradition, Adaptation, Innovation

The persistence over time of a conspiratorial style is surprising, to the point that we could speak of an entire essay subgenre and an argumentative strategy that resurface cyclically around certain events. CT historians have shown that the conspiracy stories around the 2008 economic crisis take up the battery of arguments that were already used in theories dreamed up in the Great Depression. Theories about the 9/11 attacks being an inside job orchestrated by the US administration to justify its operations in the Middle East (the *9/11 Truth* movement) replicate those that were formulated against the Roosevelt administration, in the sense that the attack on Pearl Harbor was a false flag operation designed to force US participation in World War II. Theories about the sinister intentions of Green Peace, Amnesty International and other environmental NGOs or in defense of Western human rights that are disseminated in post-communist countries of Eastern Europe recall the pamphlets on the conspiracies of Jews, Freemasons, Jesuits or the Illuminati, which circulated during the nineteenth and early twentieth centuries (Byford, 2011: 5). And the CTs on the corona virus resuscitate arguments that we already read at the very beginning of the expansion of AIDS, Zika and Ebola, some of them contradicting each other: nonexistence of the virus and the toxicity of the treatment itself, ineffectiveness of prevention measures, the human manufacture of the virus as a biological weapon, among others (Islam et al., 2020).

CT rhetoric employs two strategies to gain legitimacy and to refute the official discourse. One is to wield presumed scientific evidence: the discovery of new data, the support of supposed experts in academia and research centers with the specific terminology of the field and following the usual protocols and methods. The other consists in only asking questions which have apparently never been asked before, and doing this in an insidious way, presupposing the concealment of data or the manipulation of the same by the institutions that write official history, so that the burden of proof falls on them (Oswald, 2016).

However, two features seem novel at the beginning of the twenty-first century:

1   Although crisis situations, profound changes, instability or uncertainty are the ideal breeding ground for CTs, our time seems prone to casting a conspiratorial shadow over almost any event of a certain scope: the death of a public figure, a terrorist attack, a plane crash, an armed conflict. It is not even necessary that it be an event of a certain scope, because causality can always replace chance in conspiracy logic: a meteorological phenomenon (Hurricane Irma), some military maneuvers (the Jade Helm operation in seven states of the USA in 2015 during Obama's term),

the delusional interpretation of some emails between politicians (during the campaign of Hillary Clinton for the Democratic nomination), a random fire due to a short circuit (the Cathedral of Notre Dame in the summer of 2019) can unleash CTs of enormous proportions. The hurricane would be a US weather weapon. The maneuvering, a plan to impose martial law on a Republican and wayward state like Texas and perpetuate Obama in power, with Wall-Marts as concentration camps and Blue Bell ice cream trucks as mobile morgues. The emails were coded messages that concealed a plot of pedophile politicians whose center of operations was a pizzeria in Washington, Comet Ping-Pong: 'CP' meant 'child pornography', not 'cheese pizza'. Finally, the fire was an attack on a temple of Christendom by radical Islamists.

The proliferation of CTs worsens a phenomenon already described by researchers: fans of conspirational thinking are likely to believe in several or many CTs, even if they are not related to each other: to believe that it was the FBI that planned and executed the murder of Martin Luther King and also that climate change is a hoax. Even more surprisingly, it has been shown that belief in one CT makes the subject more likely to believe another CT, even when the two are contradictory: those who believe that Diana of Wales faked her own death are more likely to alternatively believe that she was murdered, or those who believe that Bin Laden was already dead when the US special forces entered his bunker are also subjects willing to believe that he is still alive (Wood et al., 2012).

2   However, although closely related to the former, CTs are plausible for a wider range of citizens than in the past, when they were only supported by the most radical ends of the political spectrum. In other words: we have passed the phase of *fusion paranoia* (Kelly, 1995; Knight, 2000; Marmura, 2014), whereby extremes meet, although they may disagree on their causes and ends. Globalization, for example, has unleashed the conspiratorial suspicions of both extremes: for some, it is to extend the dominance of capitalism and the market to the entire planet, and for others, it is to establish a planned economy that threatens individual freedoms and the autonomy of Nation-States. The far-right *North American Militia* cites Noam Chomsky profusely and the Italian New Right mixes De Maistre with Gramsci. The conspiracy website *InfoWars* simultaneously defends alt-right causes, such as the defense of the right to carry weapons (and the conspiracy suspicion that mass massacres committed by individuals, such as that of Sandy Hook

School, were federal hoaxes with nobody killed or wounded at all in order to promote the abolition of the laws that protect the right to possess weapons), with CT more typical of the left, such as the idea that the US should renounce imposing itself globally by resorting to tactical wars. Now, what we are experiencing is a *democratization* of conspiracy thinking. It seems that CTs have also entered a *pandemic* phase: the demographic bandwidth of those affected by conspiracy thinking increases, as we will see through data.

In 2004, a poll showed that 49% of New Yorkers thought that officials of the American administration were aware of the terrorist plans of 9/11 and deliberately did nothing about it. Another 2006 survey, this time of a sample of more than 1,000 US citizens, indicated that 36% of the population accepted the claim that federal agents participated in the attacks on the Twin Towers or did nothing to prevent them and 16% considered that the collapse of the towers was most likely accelerated by explosives secretly placed in the buildings (with a significant majority of Democratic voters in favor) (Stempel et al., 2007). Those who hold these theories were called *truthers*, because they claim to know the truth about what happened on 9/11. They are politically closer to the left and suspect that the attacks served as the perfect excuse to unleash a war against terrorism on a planetary scale that did not distinguish, interestedly, between Islam and violent extremist jihadism and to impose measures of surveillance and repression in North America itself.

In 2008 *birtherism* was the trendy CT. According to this, Obama was not born in USA, but in Kenya, and also professed the faith of Allah, which led to the conspiracy subgenre of 'stealth Jihad': Obama secretly advocated turning the US into a Muslim Republic and imposing Sharia on the population (Spencer, 2008, and Geller & Spencer, 2010, support this thesis). According to a 2010 Pew Research Center poll and after almost two years in office, 18% of Americans believed that Obama was Muslim, and in 2012 the figure was still 17%. Another survey conducted by the Public Religion Research Institute in 2011 showed that 22% of citizens believed that Muslims in the US intended to establish Sharia as fundamental law, and 31% of Republicans and 15% of Democrats believed this.

A study published in April 2020 analyzed the prevalence of two CTs very popular back then in the US: (a) that the magnitude of the coronavirus pandemic was being exaggerated to harm President Trump and (b) that the virus had been artificially created and released on purpose; 29% of those surveyed agreed or strongly agreed with the first and 31% with the second. As expected, (a) is strongly associated with the informant's political affinity variable, but (b) shows only a slight, insignificant majority of conservative supporters. In both cases, the variables related to income, educational level, gender, religion and race are indifferent. The study notes that one of the most disturbing factors is the following: 'when party leaders and media personalities promote conspiracy theories and misinformation, like minded individuals exposed to this rhetoric are more likely to adopt these ideas'. Thus, the fact that President Trump sometimes referred to COVID-19 as 'their [Democrats] new hoax' certainly helped to give the first CT credibility (Uscinski et al., 2020: 3).

Both features—broadening of the spectrum of explained phenomena and of the sociological spectrum convinced of the credibility of these explanations—seem difficult to dissociate from the emergence of the Internet and in particular of social media mixed with computational propaganda (Woolley, 2017) and junk or fake news (Venturini, 2019). One of the most obvious manifestations of the new information disorder (Wardle & Derakhshan, 2017) is precisely the unusual virulence and demographic expansion of CTs, correlated, in turn, with the widening of the band of political polarization (Sunstein, 2014; Bounegru et al., 2017).

Conspiracies and *Conspiranoias*

The existence of CTs does not mean that all conspiracies are a pure paranoid invention and that they cannot be studied legitimately and rigorously. Umberto Eco was one of those who thought more intelligently about conspiracies and CT, and not only in his essays (2017) but also in his novels. He includes them in many of his narratives, in particular in *Foucault's Pendulum* (1988*)*, *The Prague Cemetery* (2010) and *Number Zero* (2015) (Rodríguez-Ferrándiz, 2019). However, it is often true that the line that separates them can be fragile. In general terms, we could say that authentic conspiracies are (1) fallible; (2) they have a limited scope in space (they are not universal); (3) they are perishable, that is, they are also limited in time: that of their planning and implementation (whether successful or frustrated); and (4) they are subject to the unforeseen, to chance. CTs, however, are infallible, universal, persistent and subject to an implacable causal logic.

Nevertheless, we should be cautious, because the distinction is far from being so clear. If we return to the definitions of CT provided in the previous section, it can be seen that while the first (Swami et al.,

2014) speaks of 'false beliefs', the second (Sunstein, 2014) does not assign any truth value to said theories. Some authors speak on the one hand of *justified* CTs and on the other of *demonstrably false, harmful and epistemologically unjustified* CTs (Sunstein & Vermeule, 2009). Others even affirm that CTs have greater explanatory power than official history and that they are more rational, since they aspire to a totality that does not leave *errant data* without justification (Keeley, 2006). There are those who think that they are even necessary, as in Thomas Pynchon's *creative paranoia* (in fiction, however) (Pigden, 2007; Dentith, 2014). One of the drawbacks of the term is precisely this ambiguous nature. In this work, we will refer to CT as a specific way of theorizing about alleged conspiracies that contravene basic norms of deliberative democracy and/or the claims of science (Byford, 2011).

There are three features that, when produced together, lead us to suspect that a CT is a theory in this precise sense (Baden & Sharon, 2020): those who denounce the CT, (1) overvalue the power of the conspirators, believing that they are able to foresee scenarios, plan actions and gather resources outside of any reasonable estimate; (2) establish a Manichean division between good and evil, disregard the fine analysis of reality and the complexity of democratic pluralism and encourage simplifying polarization and even violent action against adversaries; and (3) proceed from a faulty epistemology: The explanations do not conform to verifiable evidence, but rather certain data are selected and presented in such a way that they are adapted to an explanation prior to any data. That is to say, these data are adapted to a prejudice. CTs are not open to criticism, because their critics would be the very conspirators themselves or their accessories. If no evidence is found for what they claim, it is due to a monstrous operation of concealment, censorship and intoxication: an *epistemic vaccine*. The plot massively manipulates information, controls political, economic, educational and judicial bodies as well as the media, to the point that they present the evidence of these conspiracies as fake news. For example, facts and data demonstrate the evidence for global warming, but there are a few politicians and celebrities and some scientists (a very low-skilled minority) who deny this (Oreskes & Conway, 2010; Uscinski et al., 2017).

Skepticism or denial finds their justification in their own weakness. The important thing is to sow doubt in the face of any hint of suspicious unanimity, to make dissent go viral and present itself as the victim of a spiral of silence, to attract the immediate attention of the media, on an equal footing (because minorities deserve visibility) with accredited theses. A misunderstood objectivity and balance of the media causes an unusual visibility and respectability for supporters of CTs and a spiral of silence and/or openly opposed to the scientific consensus (Boykoff & Boykoff, 2004; McIntyre, 2018: 17–34; 77–85). Some CTs are almost harmless, although very resistant to any evidence, such as that which maintains that the 1969 moon landing was a hoax (Swami et al., 2013). But there are also more disturbing conspiracies. The origin of the AIDS virus (Ford et al., 2013), the link between vaccines and autism (Jolley & Douglas, 2017) or the *true* intellectual authorship of the jihadist attacks of 9/11 (argued by Meyssan, 2002, and Fetzer, 2007, dismantled by Fenster, 2008: 233–278). The witch hunt unleashed by Senator McCarthy had conspiracy overtones, and was promoted and carried out from legitimate democratic power. We can also describe as *conspiranoic* the Trump administration insisting on the existence of a ghostly Deep State of officials with Democratic affiliation dedicated to secretly sabotaging government policies, in addition to promoting and covering up a monstrous network of child kidnappers and pedophiles (the Pizzagate case was just the tip of the iceberg). This Deep State was, of course, also deemed to be responsible for the massive electoral fraud that gave victory to Biden or for secretly promoting the *Great Replacement* or *White Genocide*, by which certain elite are replacing the white population with Muslims in Europe or Hispanics in the US in a surreptitious invasion (QAnon is the name that gathers the followers of these CTs on the net). The effervescence of conspiratorial thinking does not cease to speculate and does not stop even in the face of authentic conspiracies: the attacks in New York and Madrid in 2001 and 2004 were overinterpreted in a paranoid fashion, identifying perpetrators other than those proven to be guilty or the most likely perpetrators (the Jihad terrorists).

Plandemic Gospels

The most recent CTs have emerged, unsurprisingly, in connection with the COVID-19 crisis. As early as February 2, 2020, when it was still largely confined to China with just over 14,000 confirmed cases and only 100 outside the country, the WHO warned that the pandemic had produced 'a massive "infodemic"—an over-abundance of information, some accurate and some not, which makes it difficult for people to find reliable sources and reliable guidance when they need it' (WHO, 2020). It was David Rothkopf who coined the portmanteau *infodemics* in May 2003, on the subject of another epidemic: SARS. He defined infodemic as 'some facts, mixed with fear, speculation and rumors, amplified and rapidly transmitted around the world by modern information technologies'.

The increase in the consumption of communication media, both legacy media and social media, during the months of home confinement which affected half of the world's population, is a contrasted and absolutely logical fact. We could even speculate with the idea of a kind of *compensatory effect*: the non-exposure to the COVID-19 virus during the confinement has exposed us, in return, to other viruses of an informational nature. To avoid the pandemic, we have submitted to the infodemic, and the infodemic, in turn, has been nourished by the very sensitive 'pandemic' content and become viral (Rodríguez-Ferrándiz et al., 2021). The lack of physical contact multiplied the acceleration and intensity of digital interaction, so that with more days of confinement, more WhatsApp groups and more messages crossed and shared, more Facebook friends and more likes, more photos and videos and more Instagram followers, more tweets and retweets. The more social distance, the more social networks. It seems that the pandemic crisis has been a breeding ground for the 8Ps or reasons for misinformation identified by First Draft (Wardle & Derakhshan, 2017): poor journalism, parody, provocation, passion, partisanship, profit, power or political influence and propaganda. We believe two more Ps have been added to the original 8, and these are characteristic of the health crisis: panic and paranoia.

Artificial, of Course, but Accident or Bacteriological Warfare?

When the virus began to spread through Hubei, an article in the British tabloid *Daily Mail* on January 23 warned about the proximity between the fish market of Wuhan, capital of that region and supposed focus of the virus, and the Institute of Virology of the same city, which houses a maximum security laboratory with the most dangerous pathogens, such as Ebola and severe acute respiratory syndrome (SARS). The tabloid echoed statements by a scientist (never before pronounced with such forcefulness), according to which (Rahhal, 2020):

> Regulations for animal research -especially that conducted on primates- are much looser in China than in the US and other Western countries, meaning these studies are less costly and face fewer barriers that could limit or slow them. [...] Studying the behaviour of a virus like 2019-nCoV and developing treatments or vaccines for it requires infecting these research monkeys, an important step before human testing. Monkeys are unpredictable though, warned Ebright. 'They can run, they can scratch they can bite, ' he said, and the viruses they carry would go where their feet, nails and teeth do.

The scientist is one of the few who prefers not to pronounce on whether the origin of the virus is natural or not, but his outstanding words seem to refer to the imaginary plots of films like *28 days later,* directed by Danny Boyle in 2002: a laboratory chimpanzee infected with a virus that escapes from its cage and bites one of the scientists, triggering a zombie apocalypse.

A month later, an article in another tabloid, in this case the American *New York Post* (February 22), also took for granted the practice of Chinese researchers of selling specimens subjected to laboratory experiments on the animal market (Mosher, 2020):

> Add to this China's history of similar incidents. Even the deadly SARS virus has escaped — twice — from the Beijing lab where it was (and probably is) being used in experiments. Both 'man-made' epidemics were quickly contained, but neither would have happened at all if proper safety precautions had been taken. And then there is this little-known fact: Some Chinese researchers are in the habit of selling their laboratory animals to street vendors after they have finished experimenting on them.

The paragraph mixes contrasted or plausible facts (that accidents may have occurred in China) with others described in a misleading way: epidemics resulting from the escape of viruses could be described as 'man-made' (the accident was a human error), but what is suggested in the text is that the viruses themselves were manufactured products, when it seems more consistent to think that they were of natural origin, like COVID-19 itself.

Almost simultaneously (from China with love), another explanation also spread, but in this case in the opposite direction: the virus had been synthesized in a US laboratory and brought to China to weaken its booming economy. The fact that Iran was for a few weeks the second country with the highest incidence supported the thesis of bacteriological warfare. The *People's Daily,* an organ of the Chinese Communist Party, fuelled this theory by reproducing a story that appeared in the *Global Times* newspaper (no longer available online) on February 22. It said (*People's Diary,* 2020):

> A report from a Japanese TV station that suspected some of the 14,000 Americans died of influenza may have unknowingly [sic] contracted the coronavirus has gone viral on Chinese social media, stoking fears and speculations in China that the coronavirus may have originated in the U.S. The report, by TV Asahi Corporation

of Japan, suggested that the US government may have failed to grasp how rampant the virus had gone [sic] on US soil.

It was recalled that the city of Wuhan hosted a kind of military Olympics between October 18 and 27, in which soldiers from all over the world competed, and it was suggested that 'the US delegates brought the coronavirus to Wuhan, and some mutation occurred to the virus, making it more deadly and contagious, and causing a widespread outbreak this year'. The news spread in the West through a Canadian portal with a well-established fame for conspiracy, *Global Research*. Michel Chossudovsky, director of the Center for Research on Globalization, the institution responsible for the *Global Research* site, is a notable conspiracy theorist, who maintained that the 9/11 attacks had been planned by the Central Intelligence Agency (CIA); that Bin Laden was himself an agent of the CIA; and that the Western secret services, including MI5 and Mossad, support Islamic State in Iraq and Syria (ISIS). It also fuels Holocaust denier theories. The editor of the news, Larry Romanoff (2020), said he echoed information that appeared on television in Japan and Taiwan, according to which all began with a leak of infectious agents in the military laboratory at Fort Detrick in Maryland. The title of the text was an insidious question, in line with well-known conspiracy rhetoric: 'China's Coronavirus: A Shocking Update. Did The Virus Originate in the US?'.

These mutual accusations almost led to a serious diplomatic incident. On March 12, the spokesman for the Chinese Foreign Minister urged the US government to 'be transparent' regarding its involvement in the origin of the virus, citing as a source the Canadian page prone to CTs already mentioned, while Trump modified his initial words of support and praise for the actions of the Chinese authorities and introduced the term 'Chinese virus' in his press conferences and tweets, thereby rekindling the racist cliché of the 'Yellow Danger' that was embodied in fiction by the character of Fu-Manchu.

A report by Chinese virologist Li-Meng Yan uploaded to the Rule of Law Society website, titled 'Unusual characteristics of the SARS-CoV-2 genome, suggesting sophisticated laboratory modification rather than natural evolution and delineation of its synthetic pathway probable', gave credence to Trump's thesis, despite not being published in a scientific journal. The Rule of Law Society website was founded by Chinese billionaire Guo Wengui, persecuted for corruption in China, and Steve Bannon, an alt-right guru who led the Trump campaign in 2016 and was arrested in 2020 for defrauding donation money for the building of the wall between the US and Mexico. The general press of reference, such as *The Wall Street Journal* (Areddy, March 26, 2020) or the specialized press such as *Politico* (Boswell, April 4, 2020), were in charge of refuting the hoaxes related to artificial origin (whether released on purpose or accidentally). But evidence to the contrary was also in scientific literature. The journal *Nature* published an article by virologist Kristian Andersen which explained how it is impossible, given the nature of COVID-19, its genome sequence, for it to be an artificial product (Andersen et al., 2020). If it were artificial, a mixture of known viruses would be expected, but COVID-19 has unprecedented, non-synthesizable peculiarities and it has similarities with viruses that affected pangolins and bats, so the most reasonable hypothesis is that the virus passed from animal to person (a zoonosis). COVID-19, therefore, is a new type of virus, from the Coronavidae family, related to SARS and Middle East respiratory syndrome (MERS) and, like them, of natural origin, as another study by *The Lancet* points out (Roujian et al., 2020). But who can possibly believe something that comes from such Kristian Andersen? A fairy tale for grownups?

Long Distance Propagation: 5G

One of the most widespread CTs on the origin of the virus is that which relates the pandemic to the implementation of 5G technology in mobile telephones (Ahmed et al., 2020). This is the adaptation of a much older CT, which had already been affirming without scientific evidence that the low intensity electromagnetic waves generated by mobile phones and Wi-Fi networks affect people's health, being able to cause infertility, neurological diseases or cancer. Ergo, the pandemic has been caused by the 5G that many of us already carry in our pockets, on our mobile phones. A corollary of this CT affirms that the confinement of a large part of the population due to the prevention of contagion has actually served to accelerate the installation of towers of this cellular technology. These theories were released by the British tabloid *Daily Star* on March 26 ('Coronavirus: Fears that 5G Wi-Fi networks could be acting as an "accelerator" of disease'), although on April 9 the headline was modified ('Coronavirus: Activists in bizarre claim affirm that 5G could be acting as an "accelerator" of diseases') to attend to the indications of the British Government about the inaccuracy of this data, following the guidelines of the British National Health Service and the World Health Organization (WHO) (Bateman, 2020). As early as January 2020, sabotage of mobile phone masts was reported, particularly in Great Britain, where dozens of them were burned or brought down.

According to different versions of the same story, 5G technology depresses the human immune system, facilitating contagion, or it serves the purposes of propagation, since viruses could be transmitted through electromagnetic waves, transporting them distances that obviously the microparticles or the aerosols that we expel do not reach when we breathe or speak: the viral load travels further and faster than expected, thanks to wireless networks (social distance is a nonsense!!!).

Both theories seem to contradict any scientific evidence. The low frequency of 5G technology is unable to affect cell DNA. The CT usually cites a study from 2011, but this study did not prove that bacteria, let alone viruses, emit electromagnetic waves (the hypothesis that would serve as the idea that viruses can be spread through waves) and even less that they can be transported by individuals (Schraer & Lawrie, 2020). And that's not to mention that these theories do not explain how the global reach of the pandemic is possible even in areas of the world that do not have 5G technology, or how countries very advanced in this technology, such as South Korea, have been among the least hit.

This CT, in another of its 'scientifically' armed versions, has now tried to dive retrospectively into other pandemics suffered by Humanity and has concluded that all have been caused by a *quantum leap* in the electrification of the Earth: that of 1918, the so-called Spanish flu, was due to the introduction of radio waves throughout the world the previous year. The current pandemic in Wuhan occurred because this Chinese region was the first to implement 5G. Both statements are demonstrably false, but the author of this strange theory, Dr. Thomas Cowan, posted on YouTube on March 12, 2020, a video (already removed by the platform) in which he supported this thesis. According to Dr. Cowan, an experiment carried out in Boston during the 1918 flu showed that the mucous membranes of an infected person did not infect other subjects when they were implanted, so the cause could not be viral, and hence the alternative explanation, as invisible to the eye as viruses: electromagnetic waves. If we believe in viruses without seeing them, why should we not believe in these?

And thus the ineffectiveness of vaccines or simply their highly harmful nature linked to another CT dating from the 1990s which stated that vaccines are the cause of high rates of autism allegedly linked to their general administration. The first person to make this theory popular was the English doctor Andrew Wakefield, who published studies on the matter. These were later discredited in scientific media, and he was found guilty in court of a lack of professional ethics and expelled from the medical profession. However, his writings have found prominence in a very active online resistance community, which Donald Trump appears to be part of.[2]

The anti-vaccine thesis was resurrected in the heat of the pandemic by Judy Mikovits, a PhD in Molecular Biology and a former researcher at the Whittermore Peterson Institute for Neuroimmune Diseases, from which she was fired in 2011 after one of her investigations was proven to be fraudulent. On May 4, she posted a 26-minute video on Facebook, YouTube and Vimeo, which was viewed by more than eight million people in two weeks before being removed from the platforms. An excerpt from a longer documentary, *Plandemic* (75 minutes), was widely quoted and shared by QAnon and the conspiratorial website InfoWars. It suggests, among other things: that the coronavirus may have been manufactured in the US during the influenza vaccine research; that the vaccine to be administered to cure it is part of the pharmaceutical industry's agenda to reactivate waning faith in vaccines in general; and that face masks activate dormant coronavirus particles that were inoculated with the flu vaccine (Kearney et al., 2020). In addition, experts, politicians, tycoons and activists involved in the crusade against COVID (Fauci, Obama, Gates, etc.) are branded as corrupt (Fichera et al., 2020). Mikovits is also the author of the book *Plague of Corruption* (2020), in which all these conspiracy plots are put into writing. The explanation that ties anti-vaccines and 5G was provided by Cowan himself: in 2018 he published a book in which he argues the harmfulness of vaccines, and in 2020 another in which, opportunely, he gives an explanation that is not viral but electromagnetic for all pandemics (Cowan, 2018; Cowan & Morell, 2020).

The Conspiracy Synthesis

And here comes the great synthesis, with the appearance of Bill Gates on the scene. In a 2015 TED Talk, now resurrected on YouTube and seen more than 34 million times, Gates assured that the great risk to humanity was not a nuclear war, but an infectious virus, and warned about the need to invest more in mechanisms to prevent and stop an epidemic. In October 2019, Event 201, a pandemic exercise cohosted by the Johns Hopkins Center for Health Security, World Economic Forum and Bill and Melinda Gates Foundation, took place. In this forum, a kind of simulation of a pandemic caused by a mock novel coronavirus was proposed. In this simulation, the original focus of the pandemic was in the Brazilian Amazon rainforest, on a pig farm, and it revealed a number of important gaps in pandemic preparedness as well as some of the elements of the solutions from the public and private sectors that would be needed to fill them. On January 24, 2020, the conspiracy website *InfoWars* published the following head-line: 'Bill and Melinda Gates Foundation & others predicted up to 65 million deaths via coronavirus—during a simulation run 3 months ago!'. The news stated the following (*InfoWars*, 2020):

> The Bill and Melinda Gates Foundation co-hosted a pandemic exercise in late 2019 that simulated a global coronavirus outbreak. They also just happen to fund the group who owns the patent to the deadly virus and are working on a vaccine to solve the crisis. On June 19, 2015, the UK government-funded Pirbright Institute filed an application for a patent for the live coronavirus, which was approved on Nov 20, 2018. Suspiciously, a Pirbright Institute 'primary funder' is the Bill and Melinda Gates Foundation.

All in all, the news invited the following reasoning: Gates (1) knew what was going to happen and presented it as a plausible pandemic scenario; (2) because in reality it was he who manufactured and re-leased the virus; and (3) at the same time, he was already working on the synthesis of vaccines that would protect against infection, with the resulting financial benefits. It may sound very familiar to fans of the Agent 007 saga, with Spectra plotting monstrous conspiracies in each installment, or fans of novels by Thomas Pynchon, Don DeLillo, Mar-garet Atwood or James Ellroy.

Fact-Check a few days later, on January 29, 2020, separated the accurate information from that which was misleading. The simula-tion was based on a coronavirus, but that doesn't mean the organiz-ers knew about the one that causes COVID-19: coronaviruses are a broad category of viruses which cause a number of different respira-tory illnesses. One is the common cold, but the category also includes SARS (of which there were outbreaks in 2002 and 2004), and MERS in addition to COVID-19. The event was real but the fact it took place just before the pandemic started doesn't mean the organizers had any secret knowledge. The event did not make predictions about mortality, nor did the patent referred to by InfoWars have anything to do with SARS-cov19, but rather avian flu, not human flu, to which a remedy was being sought (Fichera, 2020).

On March 18, 2020, during the first wave's rapid escalation, the owner of Microsoft offered to respond to Reddit netizens in an AMA (Ask Me Anything) session. To the question 'What changes are we go-ing to have to make in the way companies operate to maintain our economy and at the same time provide social distancing?', Gates answered he was in favor of the issuance of digital certificates indicating whether the bearer had the disease, had recently undergone a test or had received the vaccine, when it was available, in particular for health personnel or those directly in contact with food or essential supplies (Reddit, 2020). Furthermore, a Massachusetts Institute of Technology (MIT) study, funded by the Bill and Melinda Gates Foundation and published in *Science* in December 2019, offered promising results on codes printed on the skin in invisible ink that could be applied at the same time as the vaccines, like tattoos. The idea was to guarantee an adequate registry of the vaccine received on the recipients themselves, in order to facilitate the sequencing of the doses and therefore the effectiveness, especially in Third World countries (McHugh et al., 2019, Trafton, 2019).

Both of these true facts were transformed and melted in a conspiratorial narrative: Bill Gates planned to administer a vaccine with robotic nanotechnology implants, capable of monitoring us and collecting data from our own interior, and that it would use 5G technology to be transmitted. The Microsoft mogul must have been the secret plotter behind the pandemic, because he has interests in pharmaceutical companies developing vaccines and in microchips and 5G, all of which confirms and completes *InfoWars'* argument.

Discussion and Conclusions

The initial phases of the pandemic caused a global upsurge in misinformation or, at least, in the perception of such a phenomenon, measured in several countries around the world (Nielsen et al., 2020a). The acute sensation of vulnerability, uncertainty and distrust towards the media and political or health authorities gave rise to the production and circulation of an enormous quantity of fake news. All of this has dramatically increased the rate of 'infodemically vulnerable' individuals (Nielsen et al., 2020b). Among the misinformation pieces, CTs have come out especially reinforced: unlike common fake news, with a more limited scope and more simple and convincing denial, CTs propose a global explanation of the phenomenon and at the same time put that explanation out of verification's reach. They inoculate the virus and at the same time the vaccine against its refutation. Cognitive and emotional adherence to these explanations increases the feeling of ineluctability of social and political dynamics and therefore passivity, victimhood and the tendency to identify scapegoats. In the case of COVID-19, it also increases the levels of relaxation or denial regarding health measures. A study carried out in April 2020 in the UK on a sample of almost 1,000 individuals asked about the three main conspiracy beliefs around the coronavirus that we have analyzed here:

(1) The virus that causes COVID-19 was probably created in a laboratory;

(2) The symptoms of COVID-19 seem to be connected to 5G mobile network radiation;

(3) The COVID-19 pandemic was planned by certain pharmaceutical corporations and government agencies.

And also about compliance with three contagion prevention measures recommended by health authorities:

A. Spending as little time as possible outside of your home;

B. Staying at least two meters apart from anyone outside of your household;

C. Washing your hands more often, for 20 seconds.

It showed a high correlation between belief in CT and low compliance with sanitary measures (Allington et al., 2020). A similar survey carried out between March and April 2020 reached the same conclusions in the US (Bierwiaczonek et al., 2020).

Long before the pandemic, all of this had already been identified in other conspiracy scenarios, but this health crisis has made things worse. Jolley and Douglas (2014), for example, demonstrated in an empirical investigation that CT reduces the possibilities of a person participating in political processes, because the action of powerful, secret and conjoined forces makes any activism useless, not to mention the sense of a single vote. Frank Furedi (2005) expressed the danger with these words:

> The simplistic worldview of conspiracy thinking helps fuel suspicion and mistrust toward the domain of politics. It displaces a critical engagement with public life with a destructive search for the hidden agenda. It distracts from the clarification of genuine differences and helps turn public life into a theater where what matters are the private lives and personal interests of mistrusted politicians. A constant search for the story behind the story distracts us from really listening to each other and seeing the world as it really is.

In our work, we have been able to track several of the most powerful CTs on COVID-19 and have observed that they take on the *modus operandi* of the conspirational genre: they overvalue the powers of the alleged conspirators (Gates, the pharmaceutical companies), they resort to a Manichean simplification (Us against Them: the Chinese, the North Americans, the Colombian, the elderly, tycoons, foreigners, immigrants) and apply a faulty epistemology (begging the question, *post hoc ergo propter hoc*, undue generalizations, conjunction fallacy, slippery slope…). We have also proved that they resort to the two most common argumentative strategies: the mention of studies, researchers and new findings that seem to follow scientific protocols; and the formulation of questions or misleading statements, which imply facts of very doubtful veracity. In the same way, we have seen that they cover practically all aspects of the crisis: health, political, economic, social, logistical or geostrategic. Finally, they also support each other, mixing secular conspiratorial themes (social panoptism, curtailment of public liberties and civil rights, eugenics) and specific CT arising in other pandemic situations (artificial synthesis of the virus, rejection of vaccines, fear of electromagnetic radiation, industry's immoderate profit motive), articulating them in a conspiracy story adapted to the event they seek to explain.

Notes

1 'A paranoia heightened by the belief that unseen forces are organized against one's self or values, or against general welfare; persecution fantasy marked by a belief that persons perceived negatively by the afflicted are operatives or dupes of real or imagined clandestine organizations'. *Urban Dictionary.*

2 Trump tweeted in 2014: 'Healthy young child goes to doctor, gets pumped with massive shot of many vaccines, doesn't feel good and changes – AUTISM. Many such cases!' (McNair, 2018: 24–25; 47–48).

References

Aaronovich, D. (2009). *Voodoo Histories: The Role of the Conspiracy Theory in Shaping Modern History*. London: Vintage.

Ahmed, W., Vidal-Alaball, J., Downing, J., López Seguí, F. (2020). COVID-19 and the 5G conspiracy theory: Social network analysis of Twitter aata. *Journal of Medical Internet Research*, 22(5). https://doi.org/10.2196/19458

Allington, D. et al. (2020). Health protective behavior, social media usage and conspiracy beliefs during the COVID-19 public health emergency. *Psychological Medicine*, 51(10), 1763–1779. doi:10.1017/S003329172000224X.

Alter, J. (1997). The age of conspiracism. *Newsweek*, 24th March. https://bit.ly/2WLc1gL

Andersen, K. G., Rambaut, A., Lipkin, W. I., Holmes, E. C., Garry, R. F. (2020). The proximal origin of SARS-CoV-2. *Nature-Medicine* 26, 450–452. https://www.nature.com/articles/s41591-020-0820-9

Areddy, J. T. (2020). Coronavirus conspiracy theory claims it began in the U.S., and Beijing is buying it. *The Wall Street Journal*, 26th March. https://on.wsj.com/37PZmPZ

Baden, C., Sharon, T. (2020). Blinded by the lies? Toward an integrated definition of conspiracy theories. *Communication Theory*, 23. https://doi.org/10.1093/ct/qtaa023

Basham, L. (2006). Living with the conspiracy. In Coady, D. (ed.), *Conspiracy theories: The philosophical debate* (pp. 61–75). Farnham: Ashgate.

Bateman, S. (2020). Coronavirus: Activists in bizarre claim 5G could be acting as 'accelerator' for disease. *Daily Star*, 24th March and 9th April. https://www.dailystar.co.uk/news/weird-news/coronavirus-fears-5g-wifi-networks-21728189

Bierwiaczonek, K., Kunst, J. R., Pich, O. (2020). Belief in COVID-19 conspiracy theories reduces social distancing over time. *Applied Psychology: Health and Well-Being.* https://doi.org/10.1111/apwh.12223

Boswell, R. (2020). How China's fake news machine is rewriting the history of Covid-19, even as the pandemic unfolds. *Politico*, 4th April. https://politi.co/3aRtLPs

Bounegru, L., Gray, J., Venturini, T., Mauri, M. (2017). *A field guide to fake news and other information disorders*. Amsterdam: Public Data Lab and First Draft.

Boykoff, M., Boykoff, J. (2004). Balance as bias: Global warming and the US prestige press. *Global Environmental Change*, 14, 125–136, https://bit.ly/3hiAm6S

Byford, J. (2011). *Conspiracy theories: A critical introduction*. Basingstoke: Palgrave-Macmillan.

Cowan, Th. (2018). *Vaccines, autoimmunity, and the changing nature of the childhood illness*. Vermont: Chelsea Green.

Cowan, Th., Morell, S. F. (2020). *The contagion myth: Why viruses (including 'coronavirus') are not the cause of disease*. New York: Skyhorse.

Dentith, M. (2014). *The Philosophy of Conspiracy Theories*. London: Palgrave Macmillan.

Eco, U. (2017). On Conspiracies. In: *Chronicles of a Liquid Society* (pp. 162–185). New York: Houghton Mifflin Harcourt.

Fenster, M. (2008). *Conspiracy theories: Secrecy and power in American culture* (rev. ed.). Minneapolis: University of Minnesota.

Fetzer, J. H. (2007) (ed.). *The 9/11 Conspiracy: The Scamming of America*. Peru, Ill.: Catsfeet Press.

Fichera, A. (2020). New Coronavirus wasn't 'predicted' in simulation. *Fact-Check*, 29th January. https://www.factcheck.org/2020/01/new-coronavirus-wasnt-predicted-in-simulation/

Fichera, A. et al. (2020). The falsehoods of the Plandemic Video. *Fact-Check*, 8th May. https://www.factcheck.org/2020/05/the-falsehoods-of-the-plandemic-video/#Scientists-Novel-Coronavirus-Not-Manipulated

Ford, C. L., Wallace, S. P., Newman, S. P., Lee, S. J., Cunningham, W. E. (2013). Belief in AIDS-related conspiracy theories and mistrust in the government: Relationship with HIV testing among at-risk older adults. *The Gerontologist*, 53. https://doi.org/10.1093/geront/gns192

Furedi, F. (2005). On the hunt for a conspiracy theory. *The Christian Science Monitor*, 16th November.

Geller, P., Spencer, R. (2010). *The post-American presidency: The Obama administration's war on America.* New York: Threshold.

Goldberg, R. A. (2001). *Enemies within: The culture of conspiracy in modern America.* New Haven, CT and London: Yale U.P.

Hellinger, D. C. (2019). *Conspiracies and conspiracy theories in the age of Trump.* Palgrave, 2019.

Hofstadter, R (1996). *The paranoid style in American politics, and other essays.* Cambridge, MA: Harvard U.P. [1964].

Imhoff, R., Lamberti, P. (2018). How paranoid are conspiracy believers? Toward a more fine-grained understanding of the connect and disconnect between paranoia and belief in conspiracy theories. *European Journal of Social Psychology*, 48, 909–926. https://doi.org/10.1002/ejsp.2494

InfoWars (2020). Bill and Melinda Gates Foundation & others predicted up to 65 million deaths via coronavirus — in simulation ran 3 months ago! 24th January. https://bit.ly/3Aq0oxk

Islam, S. et al. (2020). COVID-19 related infodemic and its impact on Public health: A global social media analysis. *The American Journal of Tropical Medicine and Hygiene*, 103(4), 1.621–1.627. https://doi.org/10.4269/ajtmh.20-0812

Jolley, D., Douglas, K. M. (2014). The social consequences of conspiracism: Exposure to conspiracy theories decreases intentions to engage in politics and to reduce one's carbon footprint, *British Journal of Psychology*, 105(1), 35–56. doi: 10.1111/bjop.12018

Jolley, D., Douglas, K. M. (2017). Prevention is better than cure: Addressing antivaccine conspiracy theories. *Journal of Applied Social Psychology*, 47, 459–469. https://doi.org/10.1111/jasp.12453

Kearney, M. D., Chiang, S. C., Massey, P. M. (2020). The Twitter origins and evolution of the COVID-19 'plandemic' conspiracy theory. *The Harvard Kennedy School Misinformation Review*, 1(3). https://doi.org/10.37016/mr-2020-42

Keeley, B. L. (2006). On conspiracy theories. In Coady, D. (ed.), *Conspiracy Theories: The Philosophical Debate* (pp. 45–60). Farnham: Ashgate.

Kelly, M. (1995). The road to Paranoia. *The New Yorker*, 11th June.

Knight, P. (2000). *Conspiracy culture: From the Kennedy assassination to the X-Files.* New York: Routledge.

Marmura, S. (2014). Likely and unlikely stories: Conspiracy theories in an age of propaganda. *International Journal of Communication*, 8, 2.377–2.395. https://ijoc.org/index.php/ijoc/article/view/2358

McHugh, K., et al. (2019). Biocompatible near-infrared quantum dots delivered to the skin by microneedle patches record vaccination. *Science Translational Medicine*, 11(523). https://doi.org/10.1126/scitranslmed.aay7162

McIntyre, L. (2018). *Post-truth.* Cambridge, MA: MIT Press.

McNair, B. (2018). *Fake News: Falsehood, fabrication and fantasy in journalism*. London: Routledge.

Meyssan, Th. (2002). *9/11 The big lie*. London: Carnot.

Mikovits, J., Heckenlively, K. (2020). *Plague of corruption*. New York: Skyhorse.

Mosher, S. W. (2020). Don't buy China's story: The coronavirus may have leaked from a lab. *New York Post*, 22th February. https://bit.ly/3hwhYrv

Nielsen, R. K. et al. (2020a). *Navigating the 'infodemic': How people in six countries access and rate news and information about coronavirus*. Oxford: Reuters Institute for the Study of Journalism. https://bit.ly/2WLebNp

Nielsen, R. K. et al. (2020b). *Communications in the coronavirus crisis: Lessons for the second wave*. Oxford: Reuters Institute for the Study of Journalism. https://bit.ly/3pnFfyo

Oreskes, N., Conway E. M. (2010). *Merchants of doubt: How a handful of scientists obscured the truth on issues from tobacco smoke to global warming*. New York: Bloomsbury.

Oswald, S. (2016). Conspiracy and bias: Argumentative features and persuasiveness of conspiracy theories. *Proceedings of the 11th International Conference of the Ontario Society for the Study of Argumentation*, Windsor, ON, Canada. https://bit.ly/3pqovGN

People's Diary (2020). Japanese TV report sparks speculations in China that COVID-19Mmay have originated in US, 23th February. https://bit.ly/2WT2bsV

Pigden, C. (2007). Conspiracy theories and the conventional wisdom. *Episteme: A Journal of Social Epistemology*, 4, 219–232. https://doi.org/10.3366/epi.2007.4.2.219

Pipes, D. (1997). *Conspiracy: How the paranoid stylef flourishes and where it comes from*. New York: The Free Press.

Popper, K. (2002). *Conjectures and refutations: The growth of scientific knowledge*. New York: Routledge [1969].

Rahhal, N. (2020). China built a lab to study SARS and Ebola in Wuhan – and US biosafety experts warned in 2017 that a virus could 'escape' the facility that's become key in fighting the outbreak. *The Daily Mail*, 23th January. http://dailym.ai/3nVWQx2

Reddit (2020). I'm Bill Gates, co-chair of the Bill & Melinda Gates Foundation. AMA about COVID19. 18th March. https://bit.ly/3aMYc9A

Rodríguez-Ferrándiz, R. (2019). Faith in fakes: Secrets, lies and conspiracies in Umberto Eco's writings. *Semiotica*, 227, 169–186. https://doi.org/10.1515/sem-2017-0137

Rodríguez-Ferrándiz, R., Sánchez-Olmos, C., Hidalgo-Marí, T., Saquete, E. (2021). Memetics of deception: Spreading local meme Hoaxes during Covid-19 1st Year. *Future Internet*, 13(6). https://doi.org/10.3390/fi13060152

Romanoff, L. (2020). China's Coronavirus: A shocking update. Did the virus originate in the US?. *Global Research*, 4th March, and All Truth has three stages, *Global Research*, 12th March. https://bit.ly/3hitmHf

Roujian, L. et al. (2020). Genomic characterisation and epidemiology of 2019 novel coronavirus: implications for virus origins and receptor binding. *The Lancet*, 395, 565–574, 30th January. https://doi.org/10.1016/S0140-6736(20)30251-8

Schraer, R., Lawrie, E. (2020). Coronavirus: Scientists brand 5G claims 'complete rubbish'. *BBC Reality Check*, 15th April. https://bbc.in/2WKdQdN

Spencer, R. (2008). *Stealth Jihad: How radical Islam is subverting America without guns or bombs.* Washington, DC: Regnery Publishing.

Stanton, Z. (2020). You're living in the golden age of conspiracy. *Politico*, 17th June. https://politi.co/2WKfX0X

Stempel, C, Hargrove, T., Stempel, G. (2007). Media use, social structure, and belief in 9/11 conspiracy theories, *Journalism & Mass Communication Quarterly*, 84, 353–372.

Sunstein, C. R. (2014). *Conspiracy theories and other dangerous ideas.* New York: Simon & Schuster.

Sunstein, C. R., Vermeule, A. (2009). Conspiracy Theories: Causes and Cures. *The Journal of Political Philosophy*, 17(2), 202–227.

Swami, V., Pietschnig, J., Tran, U. S., Nader, I. W., Stieger, S., Voracek, M. (2013). Lunar lies: The impact of informational framing and individual differences in shaping conspiracist beliefs about the moon landings. *Applied Cognitive Psychology*, 27(1), 71–80. https://doi.org/10.1002/acp.2873

Swami, V., Voracek, M., Stieger, S., Tran, U. S., Furnham, A. (2014). Analytic thinking reduces belief in conspiracy theories. *Cognition*, 133, 572–585. https://doi.org/10.1016/j.cognition.2014.08.006

Trafton, A. (2019). Storing medical information below the skin's surface. *MIT News*, 18th December. https://bit.ly/2WJgfFs

Uscinski J. E., Douglas, K., Lewandowsky, S. (2017). Climate change conspiracy theories. *Oxford Research Encyclopedia on Climate Change.* https://doi.org/10.1093/acrefore/9780190228620.013.32

Uscinski, J. E. et al. (2020). Why do people believe COVID-19 conspiracy theories? *The Harvard Kennedy School Misinformation Review*, 1. https://doi.org/10.37016/mr-2020-015

Venturini, T. (2019). From fake to junk news, the data politics of online virality. In Bigo, D., Isin, E., Ruppert, E. (eds.). *Data politics: Worlds, subjects, rights* (pp. 123–144). London and New York: Routledge.

Warldle, C., Derakhshan, H. (2017). *Information disorder. Toward an interdisciplinary framework for research and policymaking.* Estrasburgo: Council of Europe report DGI. https://bit.ly/2WLMGD9

WHO (2020). Novel Coronavirus (2019-nCoV) Situation Report-13. 18th February. https://bit.ly/2WIbYFu

Wood, M., Douglas, K., Sutton, R. (2012). Dead and alive: Beliefs in contradictory conspiracy theories. *Social Psychological and Personality Science.* 3. doi.10.1177/1948550611434786.

Woolley, S. (2017). Computational propaganda and political bots: An overview. In Powers, Shawn, Kounalakis, Markos (eds.), *Can public democracy survive the internet? Bots, echo chambers, and disinformation* (pp. 13–17), Washington, DC: U.S. Advisory Commission on Public Diplomacy (Department of State). https://www.hsdl.org/?abstract&did=800873

Index

Note: Page numbers followed by "n" denote endnotes.

www.ingramcontent.com/pod-product-compliance
Ingram Content Group UK Ltd.
Pitfield, Milton Keynes, MK11 3LW, UK
UKHW020425010325
455677UK00029B/1002